AF531696

OPERATIONAL RISK

OPERATIONAL RISK

A Practical Approach to Advanced Measurement

Dr. Yousef Padganeh

2010

Islamic Azad University, UAE

ISBN: 9789380090153

First Published in 2010

Published by: SBS Publishers & Distributors Pvt. Ltd. for Islamic Azad University, Dubai, UAE
Printed in India by Chaman Enterprises, New Delhi.

To
My Wife Shokoofeh

Contents

1

Introduction

"... We should not forget that the basic economic function of these regulated entities (banks) is to take risk. If we minimise risk taking in order to reduce failure rates to zero, we will, by definition, have eliminated the purpose of the banking system."

Alan Greenspan, Former President,
Federal Reserve Board, May 1996

Due to economic crises in the 1970s and 1980s, the central bank Governors of the G-10 countries established Basel II committee to supervise internationally active banks. In 1988, the committee introduced a capital measurement system commonly referred to as the Basel Capital Accord. The committee supplemented the 1988 Accord's original focus on credit risk with requirements for exposures to market risk. This supplemented the version of the Accord named Basel I Accord.

More recently, the issue of financial stability in the week of economic integration and globalization, as highlighted by the 1997 Asian crises, played an important role to further develop and refine the Basel Accord. As result the committee issued in 1999 a proposal for a New Capital Adequacy Framework, also known as the Basel II Accord, to replace the 1988 Accord.

The new Capital Accord consists of three Pillars:

A. Pillar 1: Minimum Capital requirements

B. Pillar 2: Supervisory Review

C. Pillar 3: Market Discipline

The fundamental objective of the committee's work to revise the 1988's Accord has been to develop a framework that would strengthen the soundness and stability of the international banking system while maintaining sufficient consistency that capital adequacy regulation will not be a significant source of competitive inequality among international banks.

Until very recently, it the belief was that banks' exposure involved two main types of risks: credit risk and market risk. The remaining financial risks belonged in the category of other risks, operational risk being one of them. Recent developments in the financial industry have shown that the importance of operational risk has been largely under– estimated.

An important difference between the Basel II and Basel I Accord is that an extra risk measurement is included in the

Accord: Operational Risk. In the Accord the definition of Operational Risk is: *"The risk of losses resulting from inadequate or failed internal processes, people and system or from external events"*. The reason why it is important to include this specific risk is to make financial institutions more financially stable, while it also leads to more integrity and transparency.

The framework outlined three methods for calculating operational risk capital charges in a continuum of increasing sophistication and risk sensitivity as below:

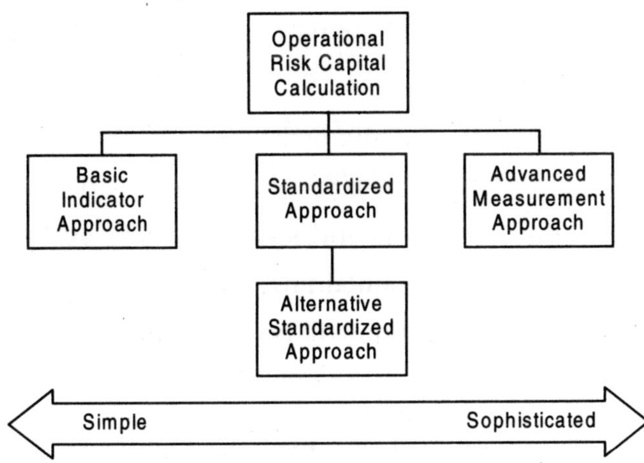

Figure 1.1

2

Basel Committee and It's History

The Basel Committee was established as the Committee on Banking Regulations and Supervisory Practices by the central–bank Governors of the Group of ten countries at the end of 1974 in the aftermath of serious disturbances in international currency and banking markets.

The Committee's members come from Belgium, Canada, France, Germany, Italy, Japan, Luxemburg, the Netherlands, Spain, Sweden, Switzerland, United Kingdom, and United States.

The Committee's Secretariat is provided by the Bank for International Settlements "BIS" in Basel (Switzerland), where nearly all the Committee's meetings take place.

BASEL I

Toward the end of the '80s the large industrialized countries asked the Bank for International Settlements (BIS) to formulate a set of prudential regulations with the aim of guaranteeing the strength and stability of the banking sector. The outcome of that formulation by BIS was an accord in 1988 generally referred to as BASEL I.

BASEL I recommended to banks to set aside 8 per cent of the capital spends for loans using a simple matrix, which is distinguished between creditors (sovereigns, banks and companies) and their geographical location. By using this approach, government risks in the Organization of Economic Co-operation & Development (OECD) area were not weighed, whereas, at the other extreme, all corporate were weighed at 100 per cent. Depending on their geographical location banks got a fairly good deal. In real term this mean that if a bank sanctions a loan of hundred million to an entity then it must set aside it's own funds of eight million.

BASEL II

February 17, 2009

The Financial Stability Institute, part of the Bank for International Settlements (BIS), which hosts the Basel Committee, issued the results of its 2008 survey into the international implementation of Basel II. It revealed many regulators have shown signs of deferring Pillar II and Pillar III progress in the short term. Some 49 jurisdictions are offering to implement the advanced measurement approach for operational risk. The FSI expects 77 jurisdictions will be implementing Pillars II and III by 2015, but says regulators are putting off implementation in the current regulatory climate.

(www.bis.org/fsi/fsiop2008.pdf?noframes=1)

BASEL II

Basel II is commonly used term for the new framework for capital requirements on banks. It will supersede the present Capital Accord, agreed by the Basel Committee in 1988 and sometimes called Basel I.

Basel II utilizes three mutually reinforcing pillars to support its approach to capital allocation:

(a) Minimum Capital Requirements

(b) Supervisory Review

(c) Market Discipline

The four principle objectives behind Basel II are:

- To promote soundness and stability of the global banking and financial system
- To enhance competitive equality
- To provide a more competitive approach to addressing risks and promote the best practices in risk management
- To provide a more widely applicable approach to the capital assessment process,

DIFFERENT OF BASEL I AND BASEL II

Basel I was one of the most important advances in international bank supervision, but market changes and increased sophistication in risk-management techniques required that the initial framework is updated. The New Basel Capital Accord (also known as Basel II) differs from Basel I along a number of dimensions, which will be discussed briefly below. In general, the framework is structured to be much more risk-sensitive than its predecessor, treating exposures very unequally depending on exposure characteristics.

Basel I explicitly covers only two types of risks in the definition of risk weighed assets: (1) credit risk and (2) market risk. Other risks are presumed to be covered implicitly through the treatments of these two major risks. The treatment of market risk remains unchanged in Basel II.

The modifications are in the definition of risk-weighted assets. Basel II approaches for calculating risk-weighted assets are providing improved bank assessments of risk making the resulting capital ratios more meaningful. The pillar one is modifying the definition of risk-weighted assets in Basel II and has two primary elements: (1) substantive changes to the treatment of credit risk relative to Basel I and (2) the introduction of an explicit treatment of operational risk resulting in a measure of operational risk included in the denominator of a bank's capital ratio.

In both cases, *a major innovation in Basel II is the introduction of three distinct options for calculation of credit risk and three others for operational risk.* It is no longer feasible to insist upon a one-size-fits-all approach to the measurement of either risk as it was in Basel I. Instead, for both risks, there are three approaches of increasing risk sensitivity.

Basel I	**Basel II**
1) In effect since 1988; very simple in application. Agreed by the G10 Focused on the active side of the balance sheet.	1) June 2004 – Revised Framework Much more complex and risk sensitive *First Pillar* – Minimum capital *Second Pillar* – Supervisory review *Third Pillar* – Market discipline
2) Easy to achieve significant capital reduction with little or no risk transfer	2) Treats exposures very unequally depending on exposure characteristics
	3) Treats banks very unequally depending on sophistication of risk management systems
=> Basel II introduced to:	=> Will profoundly change bank behaviour
O combat regulatory arbitrage exploit and improve bank risk management systems	

Basel I Capital Charges:

- *OECD sovereigns*: 0 per cent

- *OECD banks*: 20 per cent
- *Residential mortgages*: 50 per cent
- *Synthetic*: 20 per cent super-senior, 0 per cent cash-collateralized mezzanine, deduction or 100 per cent first loss (with national variations)
- *Unfunded commitments under one year*: 0 per cent
- *Unfunded commitments over one year*: 50 per cent
- *Everything else*: 100 per cent

Sample Capital Calculation

- €100 million corporate exposure
- 100 per cent risk weight = €100 million risk weighted assets (RWA)
- Capital charge = Capital = 8 per cent minimum

  RWA Capital charge: €8 million

3

Operational Risk Management

Operational risk management has its own elements, as its main goal is to ensure that there is an effective framework and measurement mechanism in place. The framework has two main needs to satisfy. It should introduce a mechanism where implementing operational risk policies would be possible firm-wide and at the same time it should undertake a process of comprehensive data capturing and measuring mechanism to assess the kind of risk exposure the firm is dealing with. Another important point to recognize is there is no single framework that fits every institution and as long as the framework can reflect what is involved that would be enough since the reality is the risk management techniques are still evolving, as they have to catch up with new technological introductions.

Nevertheless, there are key elements that have to be prevalent in the framework in order for it to be effective. The first one is there is a need for policies and procedures that will clearly spell out what direction the involved institution will take, as far as managing its operational risk effectively is concerned. The risk managing process should be able to identify risks and measure them using the appropriate tools. After assessing the exposure level, the risk elements require monitoring and overall there is also a need to control operational risk that being the main drive. The identifying responsibility lies on management that has to have the appropriate staff in place making sure that the methods applied are proper and all effort will undergo to report any loss event to make the management aware of the prevalent risk. In addition, there is a need to work on a process that will mitigate the exposure. Normally, the procedure should be firm-wide and it should summarize the prevalent exposure, the loss experience encountered, the applicable business environment, as well as well as the assessment made (Holmquist 23). Usually, the compilation should take place at least every quarter. It is also important that whatever the finding is it should be brought to the attention of the board as well as the management as often as possible, since these groups' job is to know exactly what the stand of the firm that they are in charge of is.

Throughout all this process, it is important to take into consideration regulatory requirements and the whole process should meet a minimum or an exceeding level of regulatory standard. The reason for that is whenever there is a sound control mechanism in place, it will put the management in a position to safeguard and allocate the firm's resources efficiently.

Moreover, whatever report is produced will be more reliable since there are many stakeholders who would rely on it to make sound decisions. It is also important for the existence of the firm that there is proper compliance of the laws and regulations. Other benefits of a sound framework includes it could bring down the occurrence of human mistake, as well as any

ITALY

February 12, 2009:

Italian banks are taking part in a new online operational risk loss database. An interbank consortium led by the Italian Banking Association launched the online initiative from List Group to share operational risk loss data for Basel II advanced measurement approach compliance. The scheme is part of the existing Italian database of operational losses (Dipo) project, comprising 34 member banks measuring and testing operational risk exposures, such as regulatory non-compliance, and risks of terrorism and financial crime.

(Opriskand compliance.com-March, 2009)

irregular introduction in the system could easily be spotted and traced to make the necessary corrections. In all this, the AMA standards could adjust according to the need of institutions that do not necessarily have similar needs with other similar establishments. Yet it has a baseline, a minimum requirement any operational risk control framework has to satisfy and this standard is attainable by simply applying the major procedures that are applicable to what an institution is doing.

INTRODUCTION AND DEFINITION OF OPERATIONAL RISK

Financial institutions are in the business of risk management and reallocation, and they have developed sophisticated risk management systems carry out these task. The basic component of risk management systems are identifying and defining the risks the firm is exposed to, assessing their magnitude, mitigating them using a variety of procedures, and setting aside capital for potential losses.

Operational risk is certainly not unique for financial institutions. Especially firms with heavy production processes like the car industry and firms with the complex IT systems have long been active in operational risk managements. Within banks and other financial institutions there is now an increasing pressure to manage operational risk.

Risk Briefing rates operational risk in 150 markets on a scale of 0-100. The overall scores are an aggregate of underlying scores for ten categories of risk: security; political stability; government effectiveness; legal and regulatory; macroeconomic; foreign trade and payments; financial; tax policy; labour market; and infrastructure. The model is run when events require it, and at least once a quarter for each country.

Operational risk is defined as the risk of loss resulting from inadequate of failed internal processes, people and system or from external events. This definition includes legal risk, but excludes strategic and reputation risk. The definition is actually based on breakdown of four causes of operational risk event i.e., people, processes, systems and external events.

WHY OPERATIONAL RISK IS INCLUDED IN BASEL II?

Perhaps one of the most significant examples of an observation of bank's operational risk, which is called a loss event, is the

OPERATIONAL RISK RATING

Oct 13, 2008, from Economist.com

OPERATIONAL RISK

Countries, September 2008 (September 2007 score, if different)

Least Risky			*Most Risky*	
Rank		*Score**	*Rank*	
1	Switzerland	8 (7)	150	Iraq
2	Denmark	10 (8)	149	Guinea
	Singapore	10	148	Myanmar
	Sweden	10	147	Zimbabwe
5	Finland	12 (10)	146	Turkmenistan
6	Austria	14		Uzbekistan
	Luxembourg	14	144	Venezuela
	Norway	14	143	Tajikistan
9	Netherlands	15 (13)	142	Eritrea
	Britain	15 (12)	141	Chad
11	Canada	16 (15)		Ecuador
	Hong Kong	16	139	Kenya

(*Contd.*)

Least Risky			Most Risky	
13	France	17 (16)	138	Cōte d'Ivoire
	Germany	17 (16)		Nigeria
15	Australia	18 (16)		Sudan
	Belgium	18		
	Malta	18 (19)		

*Out of 100, with higher numbers indicating more risk.

Source: Economist Intelligence Unit.

827 million pound loss of the Barings Bank. This loss event was caused by one trader, Nick Leeson, and resulted in bankruptcy. Leeson took unauthorized speculative positions in futures and options on an unused error account and started losing money in 1992, which accumulated and resulted in bankruptcy in 1996.

Among others, this incident was a provocation for the Basel Committee to include operational risk in Basel II.

MEASURING AND MODELING OPERATIONAL RISK

Most banks that are considering measuring operational risk are at very early stage, with only a few having formal measurement systems and several others actively considering how to measure operational risk. The existing methodologies are relatively simple and experimental, although a few banks seem to have made considerable progress in developing more advanced techniques for allocating capital with regard to operational risk.

The experimental quality of exiting operational risk measures reflects several issues. The risk factors usually identified by banks are typically measures of internal performance, such as internal audit ratings, volume, turnover, error rates and income volatility, rather than external factors such as market price movements or a change in borrower's condition.

Capturing operational loss experience also raises measurement questions. A few banks noted that the costs of investigating and correcting the problems underlying a loss event were significant, and in many cases, exceeded the direct costs if the operational risk.

Measuring operational risk requires both estimating the probability of an operational loss event and the potential size of the loss. Most approaches described in the interviews rely to some extent on risks factors that provide some indication of the likelihood of an operational loss event occurring. The risk factors are generally quantitative but may be qualitative and subjective assessments translated into grades (such as an audit assessment). The set of factors often used includes variables that measure risk in each business unit, for instance grades from qualitative assessments such as internal audit ratings, generic operational data such as volume, turnover and complexity, and data on quality of operations such as error rate or measures of business risk ness such as revenue volatility.

TOP-DOWN VERSUS BOTTOM-UP APPROACHES

Operational risk measurements are still a developing art form. Some take Top–Down approach, which estimates risk based on firm–wide data. These models are easier to apply Bottom–Up models but are nor sensitive to the accrual implementation to the business approach.

In contrast, Bottom–Up approach provide a structural model that is much more useful to understand causes of operational risk. Bottom–Up models involve the mapping of workflows as the business unit level, which is used to identify the potential failures and associated losses.

THE BALANCED SCORECARD APPROACH

New approach to strategic management was developed in the early 1990's by Drs. Robert Kaplan (Harvard Business School) and David Norton. They named this system the 'balanced scorecard'. Recognizing some of the weaknesses and vagueness of previous management approaches, the balanced scorecard approach provides a clear prescription as to what companies should measure in order to 'balance' the financial perspective.

The balanced scorecard is a *management system* (not only a

measurement system) that enables organizations to clarify their vision and strategy and translate them into action. It provides feedback around both the internal business processes and external outcomes in order to continuously improve strategic performance and results. When fully deployed, the balanced scorecard transforms strategic planning from an academic exercise into the nerve center of an enterprise.

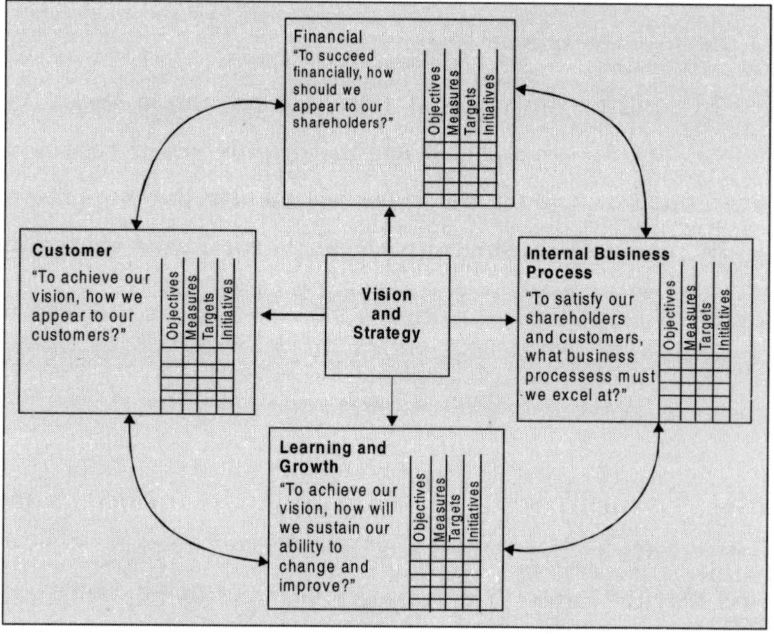

Figure 3.1

Kaplan and Norton describe the innovation of the balanced scorecard as follows:

"The balanced scorecard retains traditional financial measures. But financial measures tell the story of past events, an adequate story for industrial age companies for which investments in long-term capabilities and customer relationships were not critical for success. These financial measures are inadequate, however, for guiding and evaluating the journey that information age companies must make to create future value through investment in customers, suppliers, employees, processes, technology, and innovation."

THE SCENARIO BASED APPROACH

Scenario is high level description of artificial task that subjects might be asked to engage in for evaluation. Scenario Based Approach prepares scenario packages, exercising different aspects of collaboration across a range of domains. It sued for; Functional design, System demos, and Evaluation (heuristic, lab-based and real-world).

A scenario package consists of: Overview and task breakdown, Materials for experimenter(s), Materials for subjects, Scripts for repeatable execution, and Metrics for scenario and sub-tasks.

THE LEVER APPROACH

The LEVER method stands for Loss Estimation by Validating Experts in Risk. The idea of LEVER is that the method sues the scares loss data, which can be both internal and external and leverage it to fulfill the advanced measurement approach (AMA) according Basel II.

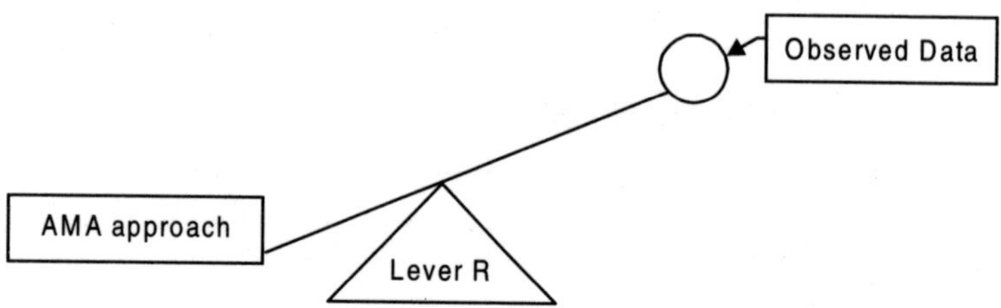

Figure 3.2: Schematic Representation of the LEVER concept, M.R.A Baker, page 29.

4

Advanced Measurement Approach and Loss Distribution Methodology

LOSS DISTRIBUTION METHODOLOGY

In all this, it is possible to say that the Advanced Measurement Approach (AMA) for calculating operational risks is better suited than others simply because it could enable institutions to have the needed flexibility to come up with the appropriate risk measurement system that works best with the kind of activity they are in, the kind of business environ they have, and with the kind of internal control they have in place. This is in addition to its being the recommendation of the Basil II Committee as one of the three best approaches to measure operational risks. There are other literatures that have studied how the applying of AMA in a given nation's financial system will be effective in introducing a sound risk measuring mechanism that would have a positive outcome. One such literature is "Supervisory Guidance on Operational Risk Advanced Measurement Approaches for Regulatory Capital" that was made available by the Federal Deposit Insurance Corporation for U.S. Banks in the years 2003 (FDIC).

According to the guideline, managing operational risk is an integral part of any financial institution. Operational risk had been around for as long as financial establishments were around. However, the coming into the picture of deregulation and globalization of financial services, coupled with the advancement of financial technology, the evolving nature of the financial business scene, and the introduction of numerous delivery channels had made it crucial that each institution has to pay attention to the operational risk involved, so that some kind of contingency plan could be introduced in advance. As a result, various nations that are members of the G-10 countries had come up with their own guidance financial institutions that are operating in their jurisdiction must follow in order to be able to use an effective AMA model as a tool to measure operational risk. The assumption of coming up with such guidelines is with the understanding that each institution has to consider its own unique complexity, structure, and culture depending on the kind of products and services it brings into the marketplace. Furthermore, the guideline stresses that risk governance would have to be on a firm-wide basis, where the measuring, monitoring, and controlling of the risk would have to be made based on how credit, interest rate, and the market risks are treated. Nevertheless, the number of banks required to participate will not be all, as mentioning what takes place in the U.S. might reveal what could be taking place in the other parts of the world. In the U.S., it is only the ten largest banks that have visible global presence that are required by law to introduce the requirements of Basel II in their risk assessment operation. In addition, there are ten medium size banks that are opt-ins if they want to participate showing that it is not mandatory across the board (Knowledge Leader).

Developing a framework to measure and quantify operational risk must be part of the effort institutions must exert to regulate capital. In order to accomplish this the Basel II Accord states that institutions should be in a position to collect risk loss data and be able to asses the risk involved and then apply their findings into a framework that it calls risk exposure. Institutions are free to incorporate a degree of conservatism in their assessment so that the quantification process will not be lacking in robustness. This is because, to arrive at the minimum regulatory capital requirement they have to rely on the existing internal process, on the required data capture, the prevalent risk, and the analytical framework that is in place.

Accordingly, operational risk could be the outcome of risks stemming from people in charge, process applied, systems in place, and external events. The kind of risk that originates from people could stem from management failure, including there could be organizational, as well as human resources failures. Factors such as lack of proper training, inadequate control, a dysfunctional human resources department, or other internal or external factors could make it difficult to arrive at the appropriate capital charge. When looking at how the process functions, a breakdown could stem from violating established processes, failure to follow procedures or processes strictly, or from not having a clear picture or a map of the applicable business lines.

A system risk could also be the outcome of disruption or system failure due to technical or other problems, whose source could be internal or external. The range of external events could also be wide where citing disaster, terrorism, vandalism, or certain events that affect various areas of the operation would be enough.

It is possible to look at certain areas that are becoming increasingly sources of operational risks, and these highlighted areas are:

- Heavy reliance on technology, which is becoming very common in the banking industry could introduce a system failure risk shifting the manual risk to automated risk, where a globally integrated system had become the norm;
- The proliferating of more advanced products in the marketplace;
- The advancing of e-banking could expose financial institutions to new risks such as frauds that could

originate internally or externally, as well as security system failure since there are sources that breach internal security to benefit themselves;

- Acquisition, mergers, and consolidation, if they are at a large scale could put a strain on existing systems;
- Technological advancement had enabled institutions to provide a large-volume service forcing them to upgrade their internal control mechanisms, as well as introducing a better backup system so that they can recover from data loss quickly (Risk Management Magazine).
- This whole arrangement would force institutions to come up with a better risk mitigating techniques;

According to the guideline, AMA operational risk framework could be different from one institution to the other. However, there are three elements that have to be prevalent in order for the AMA to be effective. The three elements are there has to be a firm-wide operational risk management similar to what was made a requirement in the Basle II Accord, there should also be lines of business management, and there should be an effective testing and verification function that will show the involved risk exposure and how effective the mechanisms introduced to mitigate it are (FRBNY).

The firm-wide operational risk management in most cases

could end up delegated to the management in big institutions, where it is important to spell out the roles and the accountability procedures. As it is applicable to any business, both the management and the board of directors have to make sure the operational risk framework is according to available resources. As it is customary, the final decision makers for major decisions in any big institution are the board of directors, whereas it is possible to delegate most of their responsibilities to the management team. Nevertheless, the board of directors has the responsibility of ascertaining that the management is capable of handling the responsibility, as well as is accountable for what would ensue and the reporting method is adequate in such a way that it enables them to make sound assessment (Kaiser, Köhne 64). The guideline requires them to have a clear understanding of the kinds of operational risks that are prevalent, as well as the involved risk that have to be considered as risk have to be managed individually if that is applicable. It is paramount for the board to review vital reports on the nature of material risks in the institution, as well as any strategic implication they present. Enhancing the operational risk framework, as well as ascertaining there is compliance with required disclosures also is part of their job. Overall, the existence of the board, as well as the management is to come up with effective risk management process that will make the undertaking effective (Wharton).

In order to introduce an effective operational risk

management in any institution there are certain responsibilities both board members and the management have to observe. It is very important to have a clear assessment of what the operation risk exposure would be and there is also a need to identify what the concerned institution tolerance level for risk is, since it differs from one institution to the other. Other issues that pertain to assessing operational risk, such as identifying the senior managers who can assume responsibilities, monitoring how the institution performs, as well as what kind of risk profile is prevalent and to make sure it is at an acceptable level that could be backed by adequate capital that is at the disposal of the involved institution should be considered in advance. Furthermore, introducing a sound risk management technique that will facilitate the spotting, measuring, monitoring, and putting operation risk under effective control should be part of the procedures from the outset.

As it is customary, it is the job of the management to spot the operational risks and implement policies, processes, and procedures that are workable and identifiable by the various business sections of each institution. Overall, it will always be the job of the senior management to come up with a method that will be effective in creating interconnectivity among those involved, where everyone would be made aware of their particular responsibilities that they have to be accountable for. The operational risk management process introduced has to be appropriate to what the particular institution is doing and it is the job of the management to verify that. As well as, what AMA requires as a testing and verification function, to carry out a sound and a timely assessment, to ascertain the operational risk frame introduced is workable, effective, and is firm-wide has to be in place. Another responsibility the management has to contend with is to ascertain appropriate staff who can carry out the operational risk function that are included on the operational risk framework are in place.

To further strengthen the AMA framework the supervisory standard requires the introduction of an independent operation risk management function in order to make sure the application of the function, the other processes, procedures will be carried out firm-wide. In addition, this same function has to be in a position to report any loss data directly to the board, as well as the management team. The function should also be in a position to communicate the kind of progress the institution is making, as far as implementing sound operational risk objective, goal, and risk tolerances are concerned. The function also has to be responsible for reviewing and reporting any loss that will be encountered, if there are external factors such as market changes, environmental changes that will introduce new risks, if there is going to be an introduction of different business lines, products or systems. Finally, the function should have the capability of compiling data and report the finding to the board and management.

Line of Business Management that is responsible for

managing day-to-day management of operational risk has an added duty of ensuring the controls and practices are in accordance with the firm-wide policies drafted, concerning a given institution's operational risk. In all this, the role the operational risk management elements play is to indicate what the best strategic direction would be in order to make certain that whatever is put in place is as effective as possible. When it comes to operational risk policies and procedures, it is important that each institution have such policies and procedures in place to spell out exactly what need to be identified, measured, monitored, and what kind of operational risk has to be avoided. The identifying and measuring aspect of the process mostly deal with the assessment of the exposure a given institution deals with. It is the job of the management to come up with a procedure that can identify and assess the level of operational risk and what the findings would pose on the institution. The monitoring aspect depends on the summarized reports obtained from the measurement that is operating in the process of the tryout to understand, manage, and control any incident that will arise from operation risk that includes a loss if it occurred.

AMA REQUIREMENTS

In this regard, what the AMA requires from financial and similar institutions is a demonstration of an appropriate internal loss event is in place. The same applies to external loss event data that should be in place. Adequate assessment of what the environment is, what the applicable control mechanism is, and an outcome showing there is a proper operational risk management and measurement framework in place are all part of the requirements. The reason for that is supervisors or whoever looks at the outcome will have to have a clear understanding of what took place, what the exact exposure is, and the other areas where if the required regulatory standard had been met.

Overall, the requirement could be stringent when looking at what both the internal and operational risk loss event data should include. There is a requirement that the institution should have at least five years of internal operational risk loss data at its disposal that it has to be able to map the loss to seven-loss-event type category. There has to be a policy that requires adding operational risk loss to the loss event database. Similarly, every loss should be categorized according to its classification to make the finding more streamlined. The same applies to external data where institutions should have polices that will require them to use external data in their operational risk framework and the management has to be aware of it so that it will contribute to the better understanding of the industry involved.

Other elements such as business environment and internal control factors need to be assessed simply because they indicate whether the control is stable or not, which would mean the exposure could be dependent on such factors where if the control is stable and fits the business environment the risk exposure could be low. A scenario analysis, which is a process of relying on expert advice and opinion, as to what the effect of operational losses will be, can be part of the data input when it is not possible to obtain sufficient data using the other assessments. Sometimes, relying on external data could be scenario analysis.

Risk quantification is not more than estimating what the operational risk of a given institution would be in a given year and the accuracy level has to be as high as possible. The procedure applied to arrive at the outcome of risk quantification should include all the factors that make up a proper operational risk analysis framework. Key elements in risk quantification are the frequency and severity of the loss since they will enable firms to use the aggregate loss distribution (ALD) model so that they would know how much capital they should put aside in order to introduce soundness in what they are doing. This is due to firms had started to combine and weigh the various inputs using various methods. There are situations where scenario analysis could play the major role in the analytical framework, while others incorporate it into their analytical framework in order to supplement what they captured as internal data. All depends on what they lack where for example; firms that have adequate internal data do not have use for scenario analysis or external data. There are others that could prefer to use the bottom-up or top-down approach depending on what they want to accomplish, but what is found to be important is the rational should reflect or justify that the chosen method is the best where there will be a need to weigh the qualitative and quantitative element. This means the accounting of the method chosen is appropriate and is required, and when there is uncertainty it is possible to make a conservative estimate and state that had been the case.

OTHER IMPORTANT FACTORS

When it comes to risk mitigation it is one way institutions could transfer the risk using certain products such as insurance, where the allowed amount is 20 percent of the overall operational risk exposure that could be supported by the collected loss data. There are certain requirements that have to be in place in order to incorporate the policy into a firm's adjustment for risk mitigation, which is not different from any sound insurance policy arrangement. The major factors looked at are the ability of the insurer to meet payment obligation on time, it is important to know what would be involved in case a claim is disputed, and there could also be a concern about what would happen if a policy is cancelled before maturity (Federal Reserve Bank).

The data maintenance that is applicable is also crucial since it is required to be effective for firms that are dealing with advanced data management practices. Firms have to be able to manipulate data in such a way that it will be possible to track event from start to finish. There has to be a capability to work on the data to modify it according to the needs that will arise. In fact, there has to be a policy in place that dictates how to deliver data, how to store and retain it, and how it is accessible in order to verify its integrity (Financier).

Testing and verification is the last process on the list and it addresses the institution's need to verify the accuracy of the data, as well as the appropriateness of the framework that is in place and the various results obtained. Usually, audit department that could be internal or external carries out the verification process where the only requirement is the members have to be qualified.

HOW OPERATIONAL RISK APPLIES TO OTHER JURISDICTION

Another publication came out in 2005 that was focusing on what was happening in Japan and it had a slightly different outlook about operational risk (Bank of Japan). Operational risk does not necessarily inflict a direct loss or profit to the firm it is applied to and whatever such firm generates does not decline outright. Instead, it is possible to suffer loss through deterioration of reputation. It is also possible that it is third parties that could suffer the loss where the victims could be customers or other financial institutions. Because of such reasons, identifying operational risk, as well as the loss that would occur when the risk materializes is not easy to extrapolate.

Another interesting aspect to highlight is it is possible to classify operational losses in two categories, where the first one is small-scale problem that could occur when there is clerical error, such as what could occur while paying a customer or while remitting small sums at the request of customers. Minor computer glitches could also fall into this category.

The other category is not frequent but when it occurs the consequence could be severe and the cause could be large-scale fraud that could originate from within or without. In the case of investment banks it is possible that an unauthorized trading could take place where citing what took place in Barings Bank would show it had resulted in bankrupting the institution. This is in addition to the known disasters such as natural catastrophes, terrorist attack, and the like. A good comparison outlined is among various kinds of risks where for example, a loss that could occur because of the fluctuation of interest rate could be a market risk, while it is possible to categorize borrowers default rate to credit risk. When it comes to operational risk it could be difficult to pinpoint the cause simply because it could always take the convergence of various factors to introduce a risk (Calomiris and Herring 1-19). Example cited is the case of a customer data leak where three factors have to come together for that to occur. One factor is lack of proper in-house guidelines about managing and safeguarding customer or sensitive information, where the second one is if the leak had occurred due to inadequate safeguards concerning customer data, and the third one could be when there is inadequate staff discipline. The assumption is for a data leak to occur these three elements would have to occur simultaneously. This will introduce a need to cover a much wider area of events and activities when assessing operational risk factors.

A good comparison is how it is possible to narrow down market and credit risk. For example, in the case of the former, interest rate could be a factor that requires a close monitoring, while in the latter case the default rate could be where fortifying the monitoring process could have a payoff. Nevertheless, in the case of operational risk, it is difficult to focus attention on a handful of factors; instead, a wide range of factors would require monitoring to reduce operational risk exposure. Another interesting comparison is the number of sections in a firm exposed to market and credit risk is limited, whereas operational risk always involves the whole establishment. Furthermore, the fact that it is not easy to manage operational risk when compared to market and credit risk, where managing operational risk in a quantitative manner will be difficult, and they have to be managed qualitatively for the most part. Finally, yet importantly, another factor considered is the effect of operational risk on customers that will result in customer loss and banks cannot handle such occurrences with a relative ease. Yet, when that is the case there could be a reputation damage on the institution forcing financial establishments and others, to consider a reputation loss is not different than what would occur in operational loss, hence they have to pay attention to their reputation in the course of their doing business (IMF).

There had, however, been change in conventional methods of operational risk management lately that resulted because of the what Basle II framework allowed after the end of 2006, where it is possible to allocate capital to cover operational risks. At the same time driver section had become common simply because the new deregulation encourages it, as well as financial technologies have become complicated as discussed earlier, where all this is accompanied with IT and outsourcing that have become widely used. Because of that, stakeholders and society expect establishments to identify and asses operational risk comprehensively. They must have a means to detect quickly when risk crops up and respond quickly in such a way that the loss will be eliminated or minimized, and they have to put in place an autonomous mechanism to manage all risks in a firm-wide basis.

The recommendation is if there is going to be operational risk management mechanism it should focus on a firm-wide basis where the only exception is there is a need to pay attention that the mechanism would not interfere with the profit-making or the expense-reducing effort.

DIFFERENT APPROACHES TO RISK MEASUREMENT

Another area addressed by this particular literature that talks about Japanese financial institutions is there is a need to quantify operational risk. It is possible to accomplish that by identifying the operational risk profile, by paying attention to specific section periodically, and by quantifying the prevalent risk. As well as, it is possible to compare risk amounts by section or business category, where introducing time-series analyses are also possible. Another possibility is to secure a capital buffer zone that enables conducting operational risk for the whole establishment. It is possible to allow the assessment to work when risk materializes eliminating extraordinary expenses whenever encountering extraordinary operational risks. Also prioritizing could add to the effectiveness of the risk management process by dealing directly with areas identified as posing a higher level of risk than others. Introducing incentives could also improve the risk management process and the incentive could come from the buffer capital. Yet, since it is not possible to quantify risk, simply because it is a cost incentive processes, operations such as collecting loss data could come up with quantitative models, and arranging the framework of risk assessment depends on each establishment that could come up with tailor-made method that fits their individual case.

This particular literature identifies several technical caveats using the Loss Distribution Method (LDM) the most commonly used operational risk quantification method as discussed earlier. What the approach specially does is it estimates how frequent and sever the loss is by doing scenario analysis and by relying on the internal historical loss data and then will estimate the amount of the risk based on its distribution. The technical caveat of this method is it mostly focuses on a few technical shortcomings that could surface through the process that will not impair the outcome to any significant extent. It is also possible to revise quantitative results by using qualitative factors that could refine some of the unstable quantitative findings so that they will be useful as a measurement tool. Furthermore, there is a stress that the operational risk quantification is still in its developmental phase and it might not be the perfect tool for operational risk, as it will be for other risks (Currie 60-100).

Another method mentioned other than quantification to assess operation risk is control self-assessments where it is possible to identify existing inherent risks and the controls that are in place. Once that is accomplished, it is possible to share the finding firm-wide and accordingly, this could enable firms to engage in autonomous risk management. It is also possible to use key risk indicators where it is possible to identify indicators that can enable an early detection of prevalent risk that is at a high level, and by keeping a close tab on these indicators it might be possible to take preemptive actions if risk materializes.

The last proposal by the Basel Committee allows banks to use the Advanced Measurement Approaches (AMA) to assess their capital charge that would cover operational risk. Loss Distribution Approach is one of the sub methods that fall under this category that are risk sensitive, as long as the data used is internal. The problem that arose was that there is a widespread recognition that relying on internal data alone might not provide what the exact capital charge will be. Therefore the best way to go might be to mix both data that would result in availing an accurate capital charge. Another key issue is how to threat frequency and severity data as the inclination is they have to be treated differently. The reason for that is the issues they raise are different. The idea is an institution that had a history of good past frequency might charge a lower capital requirement than any average bank. In reality, it is possible that the lower frequency could be a chance rather than putting an effective risk management policy, hence allowing such an institution a lower capital charge might not be appropriate.

The assumption put forward by this particular literature is mixing internal and external data will enable to distinguish which part of the lower frequency is due to having effective risk control in place and which one is due to luck. The same mixing procedure needs applying on the severity too, yet the reason for that is different from the frequency one. The reason for the severity is it is possible to avoid giving a non-zero likelihood to rare events and that might be available in the internal data. Since both procedures are difficult, there is a statistical model to use to arrive at the results. The statistical model is "credibility theory" and is in common use with insurance companies to arrive at what premium to charge. It is possible to use this model here too in assessing the operational risk and what kind of capital charge is required, as long as it survives the verification process of the regulators.

AMA AND LDA ACCORDING TO ITWG

However, a group called the Industry Technical Working Group founded in 2000 had presented an exhaustive literature on what LDA based AMA would accomplish (New York Federal). They have structured the paper around the known four basic elements of AMA, which are internal data, external data, scenario analysis, and factors that reflect what a business environ and internal control should be. Accordingly, the group recognizes that the elements fit into two groups: the first group is made up of internal and external data and what takes to capture such data and the second one is how to model the process and the integrating of the scenario analysis, what the business environment is, and the internal control system that is in place. The group had focused its work on emerging best practices, as far as capturing and integrating loss data is concerned based in what has become practical in the real world and should be part of every establishment (APEC). Accordingly, the most crucial element in LDA-based AMA approach is loss data, simply because it is the best risk indicator, as well as it could reflect the unique risk history of any institution that is doing the assessment.

If there is a shortcoming in using loss data according to the group, it is a backwards-looking method where it would fail to reflect what takes place in the environment in real-time. What worsened that is the lack of sufficient data to enable assessing the kind of loss that is possible to encounter going into the future. Such a shortcoming could be mitigated by introducing a statistical modeling as mentioned earlier, as well as by bringing most AMA elements together and rallying them to see what the result will be (Koker 37-57). The group that is made up of practitioners from financial institutions believes the crucial element to conduct an effective AMA risk assessment approach is to rely on loss data in spite of the fact that they have some downsides that will get a boost by using external loss data. While relying on the two elements of AMA, as to what kind of operational risk capital will be needed, the way to go about doing that would be to use statistics and actuarial modeling techniques. LDA stipulates that any loss a firm encounters reflects what the underlying risk exposure for the firm is. It is important to know the stance the group is taking simply because they are with the belief that, as long as a firm is well managed, there is no reason why it would not have what the group calls a well-established risk culture. It is not only that, the prevalence of such culture will enable it to minimize the operational losses.

What the group labels as operational loss is the amount charged to the Profit and Loss statement net of recoveries based on what GAAP requires when there is a loss event. According to the group, this kind of doing of things will enable those involved to introduce some consistency in their reporting. To do that it is important to come up with a category where it is possible to place every loss data of the business activities that relate to the firm. The fact that the Basel Committee has a special matrix to be adhered to will make their job easier, as all they have to do is to categorize the data according to the matrix and confirm that there was proper loss-accounting throughout the operation.

After collecting the loss data it requires sorting and whatever model is used the loss severity and frequency distributions must have been carried out separately while using LDA and one of the available models such as Monte Carlo simulation could be applied, where it is important to clarify and integrate each loss type to the kind of business activity it relates to, as well as to the time horizon. Here it is possible to introduce a curve to see what the underlying pattern for the loss occurrences will be. This curve will be important to extrapolate the amount of total loss incurred and what the minimum capital requirement will be. It is possible to choose some of the available statistics techniques to be certain that the distribution is within range. Although in reality it is difficult to come up with the best distribution fit to the tail of the data on the curve, as there is scarcity of low frequency highly impact operation loss data, according to the group. Furthermore, paying attention to the pattern of the tail is important simply because that is what the required capital will be based on.

The whole idea of this process is to determine the horizon of loss the firm would encounter in a given year so that it can come up with a percentile where if it is high, it would mean the amount of the capital the firm holds to protect itself also could be high. The percentile usually will be 99.9 percent while the time horizon is one year, as this is what the Basel CP3 requires banks to apply, except that the percentile could be similar to what the banks apply to their credit and market risk assessment.

As capital is required to cover only unexpected losses, to arrive at the amount all it takes is to read what the total loss amount on the curve is and subtract the mean to arrive at the capital required.

Another key point to take into consideration is the relationship between the risks in each of the business lines and risk type combination simply because since there will be diversification the required capital would be less than the sum of the whole parts. What this means is all a firm has to do is use the available standard statistical techniques to arrive at what would be the total losses for a given year for all the available business lines and loss event types. After that, it will be possible to allocate capital to protect the firm from losses that it wants to protect itself. To accomplish all this, the requirement is three to five years of loss data as stipulated by the Basel Committee.

INTERNAL LOSS DATA COLLECTION

When it comes to collecting data, as long the process serves the final purpose well, each institution could chose to make certain criteria a priority similar to what ITWG financial institutions are doing, which does not have to be the industry's standard. If there is a key issue to look at it might be the data collection threshold where after a certain point it might not be productive to collect loss data and that will be determined according to the need of each institution. Other issues to rise could be it is possible to come up with categories to distinguish loss events that take place in the process of data collecting. There is what ITWG calls near misses events that would have not been detected without applying some kind of a random checking technique. What this demonstrates is since the checking is random the possibility that similar errors would go undetected is high. The concern is the random check is not an effective controlling process unless applied to each transaction, which might not be practical. Because of the complication of the problems, to address them effectively ITWG has highlighted near misses in procedures applied to asses operation loss risks and anyone looking at the reports can tell there could be error that is undetectable.

Another similar occurrence that falls under the ITWG category is "Boundary Losses". Such losses are credit or market risk losses in nature, but had come around due to operational error. The Basel Committee has made it mandatory to collect credit-related operational losses no matter how they occur if the operational risk assessing method used is AMA (DeFontnouvelle, DeJesus-Rueff, Jordan, and Rosengren 38(7). The only exception is they should not be included in capital modeling, as they serve informational purpose only and it is always possible to report the occurrence already as a credit loss event. Therefore, since there is a lack of clear guidance as to what to do with such loss events, it is up to each institution to come up with a policy how to deal with them.

There are also definitional issues according to ITWG, where it will be difficult to determine if treating certain transactions, as operational losses for data collection purposes would be a good idea. To clear up such a problem what to consider as loss event is when it occurred by error only. Any other expenses incurred for other purposes should reflect their direct nature and get a treatment accordingly. Under the threshold losses are also difficult to deal with according ITWG simply because there has to be a decision to collect or not to collect them. If the decision is not to collect them, the involved institutions might find it difficult to satisfy regulators' questions regarding provisions for expected losses, as they are not going to be included. Timing also might be crucial and each institution might have to come up with its own policy as it is difficult when exactly to recognize events. Normally, it is possible to do that when a reserve is set aside for it, or when it is written off. Hence, introducing policies could mitigate such problems.

How to collect data is also an issue raised by ITWG, simply because the traditional accounting and audit method might not do the job effectively if the institutions are big and are operating around the globe. The solution for this problem is to come up with a centralized input process where categorizing it is possible according to the existing need and area of operation. One good example is to come up with geographical clusters if the institution has a large number of branches. What this enables is prior to preparing any report it will be possible to check if all sources have their data available. If it is not possible to introduce centrally processed data, it is possible to be effective using decentralized data processing system where handling and integrating it through the prevalent accounting system would be possible. Since all the books have to balance, it is a good way to make sure no mistake would occur. When it is done like this there will not be a need to reconcile the loss event database to the financial statement since the data had already been incorporated.

MORE ISSUES TO LOOK AT

A few other issues ITWG highlights about loss data collection are security, discoverability, impact of taxes on the magnitude of the reported loss, completeness, and consistent classification by event categories and line of business. The security issue highlights the prevalence of hacking requiring encrypting the data. Availing various rights of access to various groups also could monitor access. All that has to be avoided in a scenario like this is to make sure the whole process will not become cumbersome. The discoverability issue borders the fear banks have about such loss data ending up in the wrong hands, that would want to harm the bank and they might want to come up with restriction guidelines concerning how the data is prepared limiting the sensitive information included. The tax concern focuses on the need of grossing up the loss when it is not tax deductible, so that it will be inline with other operational losses.

The completeness has to do with the guideline the Basel Committee had introduced where regulators have to make sure firms using AMA have to avail a complete data. This could be difficult for some firms according to ITWG since firms are coming up with a standalone operational loss data collection system instead of the one that is extracted form the existing accounting system. This had been proven difficult simply because the reconciliation process is difficult, as operational losses are recorded in various accounts that will be difficult to track. The suggestion here is to come up with more structured ledgers distinguishing those that can be reconciled from those that cannot, so that it would be possible to minimize the problem. The consistent classification by event categories and line of business issue highlights the difficulty that exists in the process of classifying event in a hierarchy that is difficult. The suggested solutions are staff training and introduction of decentralization in data collection.

SOURCING EXTERNAL DATA

In all the challenges of collecting internal loss data, the finding is there is data insufficiency in some business lines and risk event types. That has led firms to look at external data to supplement their AMA model. There are various sources for external data collection that include a firm's own effort to collect data, procuring data from vendors, and obtaining data form an industry data pools. External data are not a reliable source as there are various problems related to them. First of all, collecting such data is time consuming, as well as there could be information gaps that require educated guess to fill or it might not be possible to fill such gaps. If the data source is media reporting there could be biases to deal with. In addition, such reports do not have a clear estimate of the cost that will be involved and if there is estimate made it might not be reliable for accuracy purposes. Relying on an industry group's data, that could fall short in the line of business and might not be the best choice because of the inadequacy of the highlighted risk.

One recommended sources for external data are vendors that know exactly what is needed and they can tailor-made their finding to the needs of firms that are trying to implement them in their AMA model and there a number of them around. The other sources that are reliable are industry data pools such as GOLD (Global Operational Risk Loss Data and ORX (Operational Risk Data Exchange) simply because they are knowledgeable in the field and can tailor-made the data according to what AMA model requires. The way pools work is, they gather data from the members of the particular industry; they anonymize it, and could redistribute it around among interested users. Such data could be more reliable and could satisfy the integrity required in association with the business type and event type better than others.

Firms also recognize what their particular risk profile is and they will not find it difficult to scale data from such sources to their exact need. In order to make such arrangement effective there might be a need to collect exposure indicators quarterly or monthly and they could either be size indicators or risk environment indicators. ITWG believes that whatever approach is used data sharing effort could be complex and challenging.

Firms that wish to qualify for AMA will have to make sure that the data they are using is complete, accurate, and covers what is required.

CHALLENGES OF USING AMA

Overall, there are a number of challenges that needs dealing with in order to introduce a risk operation framework based on AMA. The first key challenges are the completeness and accuracy of data that are vital for banks whatever approach they want to use, while they are in the process of introducing an effective risk operation framework that meets the guidelines of AMA. The other challenge is setting the data threshold although it does not have impact on the capital assessment, as long as the banks have sufficient loss data to base their decision on what kind of capital to put aside to cover their loss and what the nature of the distribution would be. The only problem that might arise is if the threshold affects the size of the available data that will directly impact the kind of capital to assign for the estimated loss that would occur. One solution for this problem is goodness of fit test that requires passing in order to rest assured that the threshold will not affect the final decision.

ITWG suggests two solutions for this problem, and the first one is to put the loss distribution below the threshold. Doing that will enable the firm to comply with the CP3 requirement and demonstrates that there is nothing lacking from the measurement applied to assess the expected loss exposure. Accordingly, the other method is to truncate the losses at the chosen threshold that will demonstrate the measure covers the required distance. Even if the CP3 requires a $10,000 or more limit, there is no reason why each institution cannot come up with its own threshold simply because it reflects the cost-benefit analysis of the collection that could be set by each institution according to its needs. It does not necessarily have to affect the creditability of capital estimates, as it is possible to avoid such pitfall by using one of the mentioned methods above.

INCORPORATING EXTERNAL DATA

Incorporating External Data could be carried out in various forms and has advantages such as enabling to complete an incomplete internal loss data, modifying the parameters introduced in the expected or unexpected internal loss data, and it will enhance the quality and creditability of scenarios. It also has use for validation and benchmarking internal data outcome.

The most important aspect of external data is its relevancy and scalability. What is meant by relevancy of data is the external data obtained to integrate with an existing internal loss data will have to have some kind of relevance, where a data that is applicable to a different line of business that is nonexistent in the acquiring firm will end up distorting the findings instead of relieving the constraints that were created by insufficient internal data. Therefore, even if data pertaining to an industry such as banks is available from outside sources, there has to be a policy how to streamline this data so that it would fit into what the acquiring firm is doing.

Scalability strictly deals with size where if certain data is obtained that applicable to bigger firms with wider exposure are and line of business, the final finding could be distorted if such data is integrated with whatever is collected internally. One way to get around this problem is to start identifying with a peer group that have similar size and line of business and avoid data from other sources. Alternatively, it might be possible to regress the data in such a way that it will be possible to see the correlation between size, frequency, and severity of losses occurred and the size involved.

SCENARIO ANALYSIS

ITWG defines Scenario Analysis as forecasting operational losses and events and what bring them about based on the knowledge of business experts. It is possible to use such a process to introduce insight into risks and mitigations that would help in calculating the required capital charge with a certain amount of reliability. Its identified shortcoming is its subjective nature and introducing techniques that will increase the repeatability rate had mitigated that problem. ITWG states that even if scenario analysis has qualitative as well as quantitative aspect, the research presented would deal only with risk measuring use of the aspect. Accordingly, three types of macro analysis of scenario data are in the list. They are supplementing insufficient loss data, avail forward-looking element in the capital assessment process, and introduce stress to test the capital charge assessment.

The supplementing of insufficient data had been the main use of scenario analysis that enables to generate a more complete frequency and severity. The combination here is interesting where there could be three kinds of losses identified. The first one is expected loss that will introduce optimistic scenario, unexpected serious loss that will introduce pessimistic scenario, and the unexpected worst-case loss that introduces catastrophic scenario as discussed (Boudoukh, Richanrtson, and Whitelaw 101). The base of the finding in the case of scenarios is opinion obtained from experts as well as risk managers, whatever the encounter kind could be. The key as indicated is it is important to draw a list of possible operational risks. At the same time the severity and the frequency could fluctuate between the three levels.

sbAMA

The same working group made up of the same financial institutions had another paper that is dealing with scenario based

AMA known as sbAMA and this approach makes scenario the center of its attention simply because the group claims that it is not enough to rely on historical data, since it would not reflect the risk that would be involved effectively (New York Federal). According to them, in order to have an effective operational risk framework in place it is important to rely on available resources that would include the advice of experts, as well as internal and external loss events. The environment and the recognized operational risk indicators should also be included in the frame work in order to have a robust model that will enable arriving at a forward looking risk estimate and risk management decisions.

According to the group since scenarios are potential future events, to evaluate them it is important to look at what would be the prevalent potential frequency of a certain risk and what kind of severity it would introduce if it occurs. What are playing the key roles in scenarios are risks factors that any business depends on in order to run a successful business, such as employees, systems, the control in place etc. since what is involved is operation and it is not market or credit that have other factors of their own. The point to raise here is if anything goes wrong with these factors, risk ensues and their not being on their optimum will end up making the business vulnerable. Once these factors attain recognition, it is possible to introduce any kind of gauging mechanism such as percentage, high, medium or low, scores of one to ten or it is even possible to use the traffic light colour, according to the group.

Consequently, once the risk factors are spotted and categorized, it is possible to outline their prevalence for a given unit in the establishment that has similar units under the same roof or line of business. Then it is possible to apply the "what if" question by integrating the risk factors to the various units. An example given by the group is IT breakdown, and if it occurs how would it affect the various units; in other words what will be the operation loss from such incidents? The "what if" question which is a self assessment process will lead to what kind of loss potential there is and could reveal its frequency, as well as severity. While doing such an evaluation, all available information such as expert advice, risk indicators, the reliability of the risk factors, collected internal, as well external loss events will be the source of the analysis made. Hence, the whole purpose of risk assessment being to figure out the potential risk factor in a given unit of an institution, it should be sound so that the decision taken to meet the operational risk would also be sound. The success rate depends on the kind of model introduced where it will have to be robust, as well as consistent, and should adjust with new occurrences by altering what the underlined risk would be, instead of the risk model itself.

WHY IS sbAMA SOUND?

What contribute to the soundness of sbAMA are the whole process deals with availing information that will meet the "what-if" question adequately, while trying to formulate the appropriate capital computation model, in parallel to the available units. The prevalence of IT infrastructure and a sound organizational framework makes sbAMA more robust and effective. According to the literature, sbAMA has six steps made up of the following:

- Scenario generation is the first step to apply in order to come up with scenarios that are pertinent to the applicable risk of the particular institution that should be consistent and firm-wide. The main sources of these risk factors are experts and it is possible obtaining the information using various methods. Trying the identified scenario events is important across the various units of the firm, as it is applicable, since in some cases some scenarios do not have relevance to certain units. When that is the case it is the experts that should have the final say regarding the non-applicability of certain scenarios to certain units in the same firm based on their experience and loss event history.

- Scenario assessment becomes the much-preferred route of assessing an operational risk when there is lack of sufficient historical data, hence when that is not the case what the recommendation in the literature is to use historical data more rather than sbAMA. Other than that the scenario assessment is based on all the known elements such as historical loss data, risk indicators, insurance coverage could also be included, the risk factors if they are applicable, and the control environment in place. Other than that, as long there is a clear guideline and definition of what should be applied and what sectors of the particular business should be included, scenario assessment is an effective tool to arrive at what kind of capital would be needed to cover operational loss.

- Data quality refers to the high quality that should be prevalent in the collected data and the assessment made, simply because whatever model is going to be used the data is going to be relied upon for the soundness of the assessment to come up with a model to forecast what kind of capital charge to set aside to cover risks that will arise due to operation. Incidents such as over or under evaluation of frequency and severity would have to be carefully scrutinized.

- Determination of parameter values takes place after ascertaining the quality of the data and there is a need to choose a model that would deal with the distribution or for the purpose of analytical solution. If, for example, it is the frequency and the severity that is going to be the parameter for a given scenario, it is possible to have a typical scenario frequency and an upper bound scenario frequency. The same is applicable for the severity where there would be a typical and an upper bound severity so that it is possible to indicate the mean as well as the prevalent deviation.

- Model and parameters will come into the picture after choosing the model and the most appropriate and acceptable model in such cases had been the Monte-Carlo simulation or an analytical model where nothing goes wrong, as long as the data supplied to them is sound.
- Model output is the final step that will reveal the risk level that is going to materialize upon which it is possible to adjust the capital charge for the operational risk. The particular literature focuses in identifying the quintile, which is the absolute value that would correspond to the arrived at percentile.

Hence, when comparing sbAMA with other AMAs such as LDA they have similarities since LDA also relies on scenario analysis when there is a lack of historical data. When compared to the scorecard approach, they both reflect any change made on the operational risk profile; as well they depend on expert opinion in order to arrive at the final capital amount. Other than that, sbAMA tend to adjust to any change quickly making it suitable to any dynamic business that requires a proactive risk management framework in place. The other advantage is sbAMA is not only dependent on scenario, it takes into account the traditional sources the other approaches are using. But, the key is how the final assessment and finding is put to work, as the rest of the approaches also use scenario, but each one of them has a preferred area that would like to lean heavily. The end result is whichever approach is used the evaluating of the prevalent risk factors will enable to come up with a sound management decision making, as well as it would be possible to control specific risk factors or it is possible to introduce a better control environment.

EXPLORATORY APPROACH

Another literature that originated from a Federal Reserve Bank in the U.S. is exploratory in its approach on how to use loss data to quantify operational risk (Federal Reserve Bank). Operational risk analysis had become very important without the mandatory requirement that had been made a requirement especially for publicly traded companies after the introduction of OXE in the U.S. and for other institutions, including financial establishments the Basel Accord, where there had been a considerable amount that had been categorized as a loss. The few losses this literature mentions are the $691 million that was called rogue trading loss at All first Financial, another $484 million settlement at Household Finance, the approximately $140 million loss that came around in the wake of the 9/11 attack incurred by the Bank of New York are among the few such extraordinary occurrences that had attracted worldwide attention. Although the need to have some kind of operational risk analysis framework in place had been heightened because of similar incidents, especially financial establishments had found it difficult to come up with effective method simply because there had been a lack of adequate internal loss data, which will make quantifying loss event difficult. This literature highlights and claims to utilize databases that are in the business of cataloging such losses and would make their data available for anyone that wants to use it to estimate the capital required to cover operational risk. The amount of capital put aside for operational risk coverage could be in the range $2-$7 billion. The literature highlights a new quantifying method called Value-at-Risk model that is an outcome of new advanced techniques that rely on computation. In this model, high frequency data is in use in order to assess what the risk exposure of a given institution would be (NYFRB EPR).

The finding is most banks do not have internal database for historical loss event even if the subject matter had been around for a while. That had resulted in forcing financial establishment to rely on the top-down assessment approach simply because the available data is mostly for high frequency, low severity, and infrequent large losses. A survey made by the Basel Committee Risk Management Group had indicated that most financial institution put aside at least 15 percent of their capital as capital charge for operational risk. That had changed after the new Basel II requirement that requires putting aside eight percent of total capital for potential operating risk by those involved that had been collecting data concerning operational losses they were encountering. The literature claims that there had been vendors as discussed earlier that had been collecting data and had been availing it for anyone who has need for it. Because of that, the literature mainly focuses on how to integrate external data with whatever would be available from within.

One problem cited as a challenge is not all institution would make their loss public knowledge even if there is a guarantee of anonymity when it comes to using the data. It is not only that if those reporting loss events only pay attention to the larger losses, the available data will be made of such occurrences only creating some kind of bias. That had led those involved to use a model where the lower threshold would be a random variable. The group claims using such a model enabled them to extract loss distribution from these public sources and their findings had been consistent to what large institutions are putting aside as their capital charge to cover operation risks. The end result had been that because of this particular model, they claim that whether there is shortage of internal loss event data or not, this method could be much superior than using internal data alone.

There are three findings that they bring forward. The first one is they are certain that operational losses are the worst source of risks for banks when compared with market risks. Second, they realize that reporting bias on external data is high and mitigating that problem will end up bringing down the capital charge requirement. Third, losses vary according to business lines, but they are not sure whether this is due to the cross business line variation or because of the samples picked. To cap it up they claim that in certain rare occasions supplementing internal data with external data could improve the risk level financial institution might face.

THE 2009 CHALLENGE: RISK AWARENESS

70 percent of UK risk managers have declared that making sure the employees in their organization are 'risk savvy' is their biggest challenge according to research conducted by Aon.

The risks companies are facing, such as increased company insolvencies, less access to credit and increased levels of fraud, need to be dealt with by employees throughout the organization rather than just at senior management levels.

According to a survey of UK businesses the key risk management challenges they face in 2009 are:

a. Embedding enterprise risk management (ERM) in the culture of the organization: 70 percent

b. Keeping „risk registers? real and relevant: 47 percent

c. Making the link between ERM and strategic planning processes: 34 percent

d. Gaining senior executive sponsorship: 19 percent

e. Making business continuity plans relevant to line managers: 13 percent

f. Credit rating agency scrutiny of ERM: 6 percent.

(www.aon.co.uk) (16th January 2009)

The Risk Management Group (RMG) of the Basle Committee and industry representative had come up with a definition that clarifies what operational risk should be. The definition is "The risk of loss resulting from inadequate or failed internal processes, people, and systems or from external event." It is not difficult to see what it encompasses or the possible sources of operational risk. The RMG has also come up with eight standardized business types and seven loss types so that those who are trying to assess their operational loss know what to focus on and there will be a standardized outcome in their effort to put AMA to work. The business types are:

- Corporate Finance;
- Trading and Sales;
- Retail Banking; Payment and Settlement;
- Agency Services;
- Commercial;
- Banking;
- Asset Management;
- Retail Brokerage.

The seven loss types are:

- Internal Fraud;

- External Fraud;
- Employment Practices and Workplace Safety;
- Clients, Products and Business Practices;
- Damage to Physical Assets;
- Business Disruption and System Failure;
- Execution, Delivery and Process Management.

The coming up of the business lines and the loss types do not only create some kind of a standard that everyone can follow, but it will also enable those who are following this procedures to share their findings and to do comparisons, which means when it is time to use external data those using it are assured that the data had been collected according to what the standard requires.

WHAT KIND OF MODEL TO CHOOSE

Another literature presented by Kabir Dutta and Jason Perry in January 2007 discusses the problems institutions are facing while in the process of choosing what kind of model to use, in order to arrive at the exact amount of capital they should put aside to fend off any operational loss event that would occur in a given time span (U of ULM). The problem highlighted is the existence of various techniques might avail a problem where there will be inconsistency on what firms could arrive at as their risk exposure. They claim that their finding shows that it is possible for the same firms to arrive at different outcomes in their assessing their risk exposure by using different methods or techniques. Furthermore, they stated that it is possible to dismiss some of the models as inadequate, either in their statistical outcome or their logical grounds.

In spite of this problem, they have also found out that there are some techniques that avail consistent and plausible outcomes for various institution that are deemed different in their business lines and structure. They stress the last finding as important simply because it is possible to infer that modeling operational risks is possible to demonstrate that there could be some irregularity in loss data among institutions. The researchers claimed that they conducted an experiment to find out the outcome of using various approaches based on Loss Data Collection Exercise (LDCE) on various financial establishments. The seven institutions they used to conduct the experiment had various business types, as well as asset size. The method they used to measure operational risk was LDA that they claimed had advantages simply because of the amount of data that was available, with a caveat that they had to group together dissimilar losses. The components that LDA avails readily frequency, severity, and the aggregate loss distribution had made their job effective and easy. Since they claim that they understood that there will be a shortfall in most of the simple methods in analyzing the data, they nevertheless went ahead and applied three techniques that they called: parametric distribution fitting, extreme value theory, and capital estimation that uses non-parametric empirical sampling. In all the techniques they applied, what they focused on to arrive at in their estimate was the following performance measures:

- *Good fit statistics*: how the data and the method co-function;
- *Realistic*: assuming that the model works effectively; could it arrive at a realistic capital estimate?
- *Flexibility*: testing the capacity of the model to accommodate a large variety of loss event data;
- *Simple*: the responsiveness of the method in random number generating, as well as ease of practical applicability.

They stressed that goodness-of-fit tests are necessary since they enable segregating techniques expected to introduce cross institution dispersion in the process of arriving at the capital charge required. Their preference of measuring was comparing the Quantil-Quantile plot among various establishments and they had found the g-and-h distribution and the Q-Q plot as good fit. The rest of the models they experimented with such as extreme value theory had shot into unrealistic ranges sometimes surpassing 100 percent of asset size demonstrating they cannot model high losses accurately. What they zeroed on is that they were able to defy other researches who claimed it is not possible to come up with a model that can find a single distribution point that fits both the body and the tail of the data of operational loss. Their conclusion had been that they had enough empirical evidence that the method they used was effective most of the time and whenever it was not effective, the difference was nominal.

The whole drive was to come up with effective methods to measure operational loss and it is becoming very crucial since the financial establishments are suffering sizable operational losses. It was Froot (2003) who was able to declare that operational risk is capable of introducing non-liquidity that will lead the financial system into a risk of a tailspin as mentioned in the literature. What this means is the need to fend off such calamity is high and that had led the Basel II Capital Accord to require every financial institution to start using AMA in assessing their operational risk exposure. Other countries other than the U.S. can use similar and simpler techniques such as Basic Indicators or Standardized Approaches. The amount of capital charge for everyone involved remains to be eight percent of enterprise-level gross revenue (Hull 343).

The other problem highlighted is LDA is a recent introduction in an environment where institutions were not at ease with their internal data and it is only recently the loss event data availability problem across the board started improving. The researchers claim that there had been other researchers such as Moscadelli (2004) and de Fontnouvell et al. (2004) who had experimented with operational data loss in recent years and their case is different in such a way that, instead of trying to find out if certain techniques can be used to asses the loss event data of a given institution, their focus had been to come up with a method to measure loss event data appropriately as discussed in the literature. According to them, their stand is not different from various researchers who claim that there has to be a sound technique that would assess the exact capital charge requirement, as much as possible. Overall, this particular literature that demonstrated various methods that would be shown in the following section that deals with some of the techniques and models used show that there is a concern to come up with as many techniques as possible that would lead to the exact ideal capital charge estimation when it comes to putting aside capital in order to cover for operational risk loss.

OUTCOME OF SESSIONS HELD IN JAPAN

Another literature is about a study made by the Advancement of Operational Risk Management of five sessions held through March 2006 and the group wants to disseminate the outcome of the session so that some institutions might use the finding to advance their operational risk management (Bank of Japan).

At the same time, the literature is essential in shedding light on how various regions of the world are dealing with operational risk and what kind of advancement they have made in parallel to what is happening in other geographical regions. The discussion held on December 22, 2005 had focused on selecting the type of distribution for risk quantification. As it is common among institutions, here also the preferred method used is Loss Distribution Approach (LDA) where the assessment focuses on the frequency and the severity of the losses by arriving at how much money the loss event would cost the involved entities, in this case financial establishments in Japan. The session recognized that there is no convergence to what it calls a de facto practical standard approach, as far as the amount of the loss event is concerned. The same applies when it comes to validating what kind of parameters to use. Although as discussed earlier there are claims in some corners where it was possible to come up with techniques that could deliver a similar capital charge amount across similar institution. This literature is claiming that it is the distribution method used that will determine what kind of capital charge to put aside and it could vary from one case to the other. Accordingly, the reason that contribute to the convergence are the following:

- There is no method that can identify the risk event at the quality of process level, the high and low frequency level, and the tail event that do not take place often.

- It is possible that the loss data captured by financial firms might fall short of representing the actual risk profile by relying on numbers, genre of samples, and the time span the observation was applied.

LACK OF ADEQUATE DATA IS THE MAIN CULPRIT

The literature concedes that the fact that the chosen distribution method should fit the data type has a deciding factor to arrive at a sound estimation, but it claims there is more that requires consideration. The point raised here is it is common to encounter similar problems everywhere, where the loss event data available will not always be adequate; hence, it necessitates picking a distribution method based on that. What the literature arrived at is if the internal data is found to be inadequate other sources should be considered such as scenario data, etc and the methods used have to be streamlined in such a way that they will not introduce instability that will render a defective data for quantification purposes.

The suggestion is to bear in mind that information on the superiority of individual approaches is currently limited, where the probable meaning might be since the nature of the quality of the data is questionable across the board, each establishment should come up with a method that fits the kind of data that it was able to capture. Here, the stance is that no matter what is involved there will always be insufficiencies of loss data captured by financial institutions that would require supplementing it by other sources such as scenario approach or external data. Furthermore, whether the relying on is in order to make up for the insufficiency of internal data, scenario, or external data, the condition to consider requires basing upon the quantification method of the implementation. What to look at is not different from what had been covered so far such that it is important to identify the scenario data that will meet the optimal quantification need, there has to be some comparison between external data, and the scenario to choose to make sure which one would meet best the quantification need, and there has to be certain degree of comprehensiveness.

Then comes the setting up of the parameters of the distribution that should fit in particular the prevalent frequency and severity of loss distribution. The other problem highlighted is there is the need to pressure management that the distribution method chosen is effective and it will not add to the complication of choosing parameters. Here, what is important is that it is enough for the management or board to grasp the characteristic of the mode where there is no need for them to comprehend the details of the model. The fact that the financial institution in Japan are using both Basic Indicator Approach and The Standardized Approach had been made clear simply because they are used to confirm the quantification method chosen is effective by comparing the final amount arrived at by the various methods.

RISK CLASSES

On the Session held on January, 26, 2006 if there is a new introduction it was what the paper called "risk classes" that are operational risk events and the reason for that was it is possible to quantify each group using premises that are particularly pertinent to them. The individual units are made up of event types, business lines, event type and business lines in conjunction, cause of loss, legal entity, and the need is to find out if converging of the whole data together is possible. The reason for that is the class setting and the impending of dependencies among the various risk types affect the result of risk quantification. The example given on the literature to support this outlook is that if what it involved is adding the risks allocated to each class, there will be a tendency in the aggregated risk to go higher. Whereas, when the case is the other way around and there is subdivision it would be easier to introduce subdivisions. The problem cited here is the number of data will go down when forming a class necessitating data supplementing. If there is a setback in this assessment it is that the degree of dependency might differ depending on the amount of the loss. It is also possible to introduce simple guidelines that fit the particular environment where the operational risk basement is applied. Another point raised is the point where dependencies are considered, which is at the time of classifying the data and when quantifying the aggregated risk amount.

THE REMAINING SESSIONS

What the fourth session highlighted was the best time to use scenario data is when there is a need to supplement internal loss data that are low frequency and high severity losses and it is important to be careful while implementing such data simply because the risk amount would be dependent upon what such data avails. If there are more points raised that are not very much different than what is already applicable across the industry. If there had been a different twist to what had been discussed the top-down and bottom-up approaches have to be present to give the data some balancing assurance, while at the same time the scenario data has to be verified before put to use.

The fifth session started out by focusing on internal losses that are historical data that might have record of recent incidents and it is important to take that into consideration. One concern highlighted was the applied anti-recurrence measures where if they are applicable might not be reflected in the historical data making them unreliable. In order to mitigate such problems it might be necessary to include Key Risk Indicators (KRI) in addition to using scenario data. Furthermore, the recommendation is to use qualitative evaluation methods such Control Self Assessments (CSA) discussed earlier, using risk control function, to enable auditors do an independent evaluations of the data, as well as the findings, and managerial judgments should also be integrated into the final outcome.

Overall, this literature sheds light on the fact that what had been introduced by the Basel II Accord is at work around the world with few adjustments made to make it a sound measuring tool as far as operational risks are involved in the global financial market. The fact that there is a high level of similarity would add to the possibility of using external data captured from various parts of the world that include scenarios that had occurred in such organizations.

FITCH RATINGS

Another literature supplied by Fitch Ratings, a rating company presents the overall effect of the Basel II implementation in assessing operational risk in the banking industry around the world (Fitch Ratings). The genre of the participants was 15 percent from around the globe, 24 percent from North America, and 61 percent from Europe. According to Fitch's finding based on a survey made among users of AMA, the amount of capital charged was different or lower than that of those using the Standardized or Basic Indicators approaches. But the various outcomes according to Fitch do not reflect the diversification effect that could lower the capital charged arrived at using AMA, as well as it does not reflect the home/ host principles introduced by Basel II Committee as a requirement for regulators to enable diversification recognition benefits.

Another area was if the AMA is going to introduce any kind of incentive for the banking industry it would have to generate a lower capital charge than the other approaches and what will contribute to that is diversification. Furthermore, Basel II recommends each financial institution to use its own discretion while developing a method or model in order to arrive at a risk exposure level that is relevant to the involved institution. The same is applicable to countries too where they have to use their own discretion in validating and approving the effectiveness of the models used. There is a concern, however, about uniformity and consistency among international banks where there is a fear of derailing competitiveness.

The concerns outlined by Fitch are directly concerning diversification, handling of expected losses, and the use of incurrence to mitigate the capital charge.

Other findings are the participants had recognized that a high level of sophistication is required in order to bring the available tools together and employ them effectively to arrive at appropriate capital charge, where there is an inherent challenge of streaming all prices of the prevalent approaches. The bringing together of internal and external data and integrating it with structured scenario had also been a challenge. The other concern highlighted by the participants was the involved high level of value judgment and the heavy reliance on expert opinion could end up manipulating the models.

Fitch believes that if there is something lacking it is a lack of open environment as the findings indicate the overall environment had been rigid and judgmental. The issues Fitch wanted to address when conducting the survey was:

- To determine the kind of process the establishments had gone through to come up with an effective operation risk framework;
- To identify what the issues and challenges that are facing banks in their effort to introduce an effective operation risk framework are;
- Asses what kind of preparation banks had made to meet the Basil II regulatory requirements, as well as how they had positioned themselves to the prevalent competition;

Fitch had approached more than 50 banks and most of them had participated at varying degrees, although there were times some of the questions went unanswered simply because of confidentiality reasons. The findings reveal that there is a high level of convergence to what Basel II termed as operational risk. The other finding is even if strategic, business, and reputation risks had been excluded from Basel II because of the difficulty they present in quantifying them, Fitch had found out that there are banks that are addressing these issues as operational risks or independently by using qualitative measuring methods to capture them.

THE MOST PREFERRED METHODS

Among the banks, surveyed most of them claimed that they were combining the available methods in order to identify risks. Accordingly, 65 percent of the banks surveyed are using self-assessment, 32 percent were using key risk indicators, 37 percent were using risk mapping and the remaining 10 percent were combining scorecards in their methods. While conducting the self-assessment, the banks had been relying on the bottom-up approach getting insight from line managers about the kind of risks they face. The risk indicators were useful for measuring risk from a top-level perspective where it had been possible to drill down to trouble spots. The top-down and bottom-up approaches were useful in capturing all events since their application is firm-wide, while the final decision will be made by top management making it effective in arriving at the appropriate capital charge, although there are still more approaches (IMF).

The structure and culture of the organizations surveyed was in such a way that either the board or senior management have the controlling lever or it is possible to vest the responsibility to a single executive such as a financial officer

(Oliver Wyman Consulting). In addition, most of the firms had a conceptualized operation function overseeing the operational risk function and is responsible for the most part for developing methods, policy, tools, and software in some cases to facilitate the process of identifying and capturing loss events. Respondents had supported as effective other areas such as including business line management in assessing risk management. In most of the banks surveyed, management had been playing a significant role in the risk-assessing process. When it comes to the culture and openness, it is only a few banks that claimed creating such an environment would be beneficial to risk assessment.

Other banks have not seen the importance of creating a culture where staff will be encouraged to talk about risk that worries them. Fitch's stand on the issue is that people have to be encouraged to come forward with risks whenever they spot them, as it will give a boost to a worst-case situation, especially in scenario testing. Loss data collection is key in arriving at the appropriate risk capital, however, the survey indicated that banks are at various levels when it comes to the quality, time covered, and the level of the data collected. The findings reveal 43 percent of the survey participants had collected at least 1-2 years of data for certain business lines and for others between 2-3 years. The remaining 13 percent had collected one year or less data. What this means according to Fitch is a sizeable number of the banks are doing a good job although most of them worry about the quality of the data they collect and they point out the overlapping with other business lines such as credit and market could result in double counting of loss events.

Other areas such as thresholds and "near-misses" also pose problems as they vary according to individual banks. The banks worry about the implication of setting a high threshold limits since low-level losses would not be included and to remedy this problem some of them have chosen to factor such low level losses as a cost of doing business instead of risk. The problem with "near-misses" is there is difficulty in measuring them accurately. Other problem cited in the survey was since process level managers are required to use their discretion in the case of near misses the end result could vary and could be void of consistency.

Another Fitch finding is 75 percent of the banks participated in the survey will want to become eligible for the AMA and most of them could qualify by the 2007 implementation date. The banks involved in the survey are bigger banks resulting the outcome does not reflect the progress the smaller banks are making. Some of the capital charges shown by the participants revel that it would higher than what could have been if the earlier standardized approach had been used. The only time the AMA might result in lowering capital charge might be if diversification benefits are recognized. This had led Fitch to extrapolate that somehow

AMA techniques should manage to arrive at a lower capital charge in order for them to introduce advantages for the banks. Some of the banks also have planned to use a loss distribution approach to arrive at their appropriate capital charge and they can accomplish that by creating expected and unexpected loss by employing a loss distribution data (Rachev & al. 22). A problem cited is most of the participating banks have only collected data for less than five years and the quality of such data had been questioned making it difficult to come up with an operational loss estimation that is reliable. Because of the fact that the banks might be interested to know what the tail of the distribution would be they have no choice other than introducing other techniques, as well as supplement their internal data from outside sources.

External data had a major role to play among the banks surveyed and they have used it for the flowing purposes: to augment their internal data, as a validating tool for assumed distribution, and to help them analyze scenario data. Scalability had been identified as one of the major challenges for the banks when they try to integrate external data. The better use external data had been when it is used for validation purposes according to the finding. Scenario analysis had been popular among the banks participated in the survey simply because it takes into account the environment of the institution using it and it is forward looking. If there is a problem with it according to Fitch's finding, it is its subjective nature where cultural issues could impede its effective application. Overall, Fitch's survey ascertains that many banks are striving to make the Basel II AMA their main tool to asses their operational risk and to arrive at the most appropriate capital charge and they are showing a steady progress, where in the near future most of the surveyed banks would meet the regulatory requirement. What this brings to the fore is the outcome is similar across the board and in the near future the consistency and relevancy level could be augmented where there will be a uniformity in what most banks around the world would be doing and that in its turns would contribute a lot in the process of data capturing, since the reliability of data obtained in the future would be very high.

THE APPLICATION OF TECHNOLOGY TO ORM

Another literature that discussed the technological advancement made in assessing OR is from CHARTIS Research that emulated to show what exactly is taking place, as far as using IT to asses operational risk is concerned (CHARTIS Research)

Accordingly, what CHARTIS calls "risk technology" might not yet be where everyone one wants it. What this means is there is a lack of a robust risk basement technology in the marketplace. CHARTIS states that the market for ORM systems is still evolving and it includes various kinds of players, large, medium, and small niche players from various industries. Without denying the fact that the technology in this area is immature and is the least sophisticated when compared with market and credit risk assessment, there is some advancement made because of the prevalent demand, but the outcome seems to be fragmented. The reason for that is there are only single systems of software that have a single usage or capability, such as dealing with Risk & Control Self Assessment, Internal loss/event database, Key Risk Indicator, and Scorecards etc. and till date it seems that there is a failure to come up with an operational risk management and measurement methodology to address the whole risk assessment issue through one package.

What had been practical according to a survey made on 130 financial institutions is 58 percent of respondents stated that they will use a combination of LDA and COSO (Committee of Sponsoring Organization of the Treadway Commission). Another 48 percent said they are planning to use AMA, while 38 percent said they would combine ORM and Sarbanes-Oxley requirements into one software application. The problem is there is not yet such effective software in the market. Nevertheless, the market size ORM would represent worldwide could grow to more than $1 billion by 2009 according to CHARTIS. At the same time, the ORM software market could grow by more than six percent and could approach $192 million by 2009.

In spite of this being the reality, CHARTIS states that when taking the number of would be vendors of software in the market the available niche does not justify their existence. When seen from individual institution perspective the expenditure varies according to their size, where the larger financial institutions have a large budget for ORM software. When looking at the size of the expenditure the Europeans banks lag behind their counterpart in the U.S. and that had been attributed to what SOX requires the U.S. banks, while at the same time most firms would prefer to combine their Basel II and SOX programmes into a single IT budget (Cummings, Lewis, and Wei 30(10).

As far as the landscape is concerned, CHARTIS claims that there is something lacking in both sides that are the available niche, as well the kind of software products that are coming into the market, although the latter is evolving at a healthy rate. The fragmentation of what the various software are capable of doing had made it difficult for the users simply because it could be difficult to bring together the various components in such a way that it would be possible to assess the risk effectively and arrive at the capital charge. This capability is still lacking and is the probable reason why there is a lackluster niche. Nevertheless, that could start changing around 2008 if the vendors manage to come up with a seamless integration of data management, compliance, and governance software systems, if possible integrating all class risks, such as credit, market, and operation into what CHARTIS called a single point of knowledge for performance management.

Currently, the size of the vendors that have a widely varied approaches have made it difficult for the institutions which one to pick. At the same time, since most systems avail a short-term solution they are not fit for any kind of long-term investment. CHARTIS advises buyers to look at the following factors while trying to implement any kind of software (IBM). The core functionality, data management capability, vendor characteristic, implementation process, interface, complexity, customizability/flexibility, and the involved cost should be studied thoroughly before investing on any system. What the reality is most firms are using the traditional qualitative approach although some are trying to introduce some use of software. Those using system software are finding it difficult to find out if what they are doing is correct, simply because there is no guideline about how the regulators are going to evaluate assessments done using software.

Consequently, that area still requires evolving where vendors would have to be in a position to come up with a method that will do all the jobs together, simply because dealing with one segment of the process, with the knowledge that there is no means of integrating them does not make sense (RWTH). That is the reason why the niche is not there although the demand is there. However, if there is an effective system that will convince all the involved, including the regulators about its robustness that it could introduce and the cost reduction advantage it would avail and is an appropriate method to arrive at the capital charge, there is a good probability the demand will pick up. CHARTIS predict that might be possible by the year 2010 and 2011.

SUMMARY

Operational risk was not a serious challenge before high-profile cases started changing the landscape. The major focus was on the kind of risk that was prevalent in the market and credit sectors simply because the loss those sectors were experiencing was significant. What this brought to the fore was regulatory control that requires observing, in order to avoid fallout since the regulators could go to any length to make sure the implementation according to the agreed upon regulations. Since financial establishments have to adhere to these rules, without considering any of the merits that will percolate their way by simply doing their job systematically, they had to find effective and economical means to implement the so called regulations. That was when it became obvious operational risk also requires some kind of a comprehensive and structured approach in order to predict what kind of capital charge it will bring around, as well as when deliberating if mitigating or avoiding the risks is possible. It was not an easy task to bring this obligatory undertaking to fruition, as inferring it is possible from what took place till now, from the time banks started to give a special consideration to operation risk management and they are still grappling with the challenge. To make things worse the regulators who came up with Basel I and Basel II Accord have some kind of a deadline in place when those required would have to start implementing the required regulation firm-wide.

The process is not getting a considerable help from systems technology as the advancement in coming up with an effective solution is still lagging simply because no one is able to come up with a solution that will make the risk assessment process more manageable than it is now. This demonstrates that there is some learning curve those in charge of software designing have to get over, which will take time even if everyone is optimistic to see a positive result in three to five years time.

Some of the reasons for that could be due to the high level of expectation from such systems that are prevalent since areas such as disseminating the right kind of information about the existing culture is important and it is not difficult to see how challenging that will be to integrate with any kind of IT system. Collecting and sorting out loss data information might also be difficult to automate. Then comes the measuring process followed by the presentation to the board of directors, as well as the management team. Here the number of groups that want to see the final tally would be high and could include various committees that include regulators, the audit team, as well as owners of business might want to know what the final outcome is. To make things complicated the system might have to allow those who are in charge, mostly managers, to track any improvement and new introduction that might involve people, systems, process, environment etc., so that they will be in a position to take measures to reduce or eliminate risks. Overall, until there is a technology that will accomplish all of this and more the job of arriving at the capital charge will be tedious, as the other alternative is to use the available formulas and statistics that takes time. It is not only time the accuracy level might not be where everyone wants it to be, although with high diligence it is possible to arrive at the best approximation of what the capital charge would be.

In spite of the prevalent problem, where it is not yet time to get a robust help from technology, the focus would shift to the overall performance of a given financial establishment that will have to show a reliable outcome for the stakeholders. It is not possible to attain such performance unless there is a means of communicating what the direction the business will be taking to those who are in charge of the various business lines in a given firm. There is also another worry, which is the direction the firm will be taking in the future as far as competitiveness, profitability, and risk reduction or elimination are concerned. When that is visualized and some effort has undergone to implement it, there is another need, which is what the Basel II Accord is trying to accomplish, as far the effort to introduce some kind of a global accord among financial establishments are concerned, where all of them if possible would share similar values in the future.

That does not necessarily mean compromising competitiveness at any level, although a synergy to work together to reduce risk is the experts' recommendation. That will make it possible across the board to bring down the size of the capital charge that every bank should put aside on yearly basis that is not generating any income. Consequently, until the prevalent problems are dealt with, where an advanced technology gives the industry and those in charge some kind of a break, while at the same time it promises to put more revenue in the pockets of the stakeholders, the existing system would have to continue to do what it is doing currently, where among other things the major focus should be on releasing some of the capital that would be locked away without availing any benefit.

KPMG SURVEY LOOKS INTO BANKING RISK MANAGEMENT

As banks examine the factors leading to the current credit crisis, it is becoming clear that risk management typically is not viewed as central to strategic decision-making, according to a survey by KPMG LLP.

More than three-quarters (76 percent) of the almost 500 global banking executives surveyed report that risk management is still stigmatized as a support function at their bank. Only half (48 percent) said that risk management is understood to be the responsibility of everyone in the organization, and another 45 percent of respondents said their board lacks risk expertise. Furthermore, 64 percent of respondents said that...

(*Contd.*)

…their chief risk officer needs to hold greater influence over strategy development, despite 81 percent of respondents reporting that risk management is viewed by their bank as a competitive advantage.

The KPMG 'Risk Management in Banking' survey, conducted by the Economist Intelligence Unit, was based on telephone interviews conducted in October 2008 with 496 senior managers at organizations involved in corporate, retail, investment and private banking, as well as asset management. Three-quarters (76 percent) of the banks participating in the survey have a chief risk officer (CRO) or equivalent.

(www.us.kpmg.com) (8th January 2009)

5

Methodology for Calculation of Operational Risk Capital Charges

Basel Committee on Banking Supervision has announced three main approached to the banks for their capital charges calculation. They are:

1. Basic Indicator Approach
2. Standardized Approach
3. Advanced Measurement Approach.

The Basic Indicator approach is the simplest one and Advanced Measurement Approach is the highly sophisticated approach.

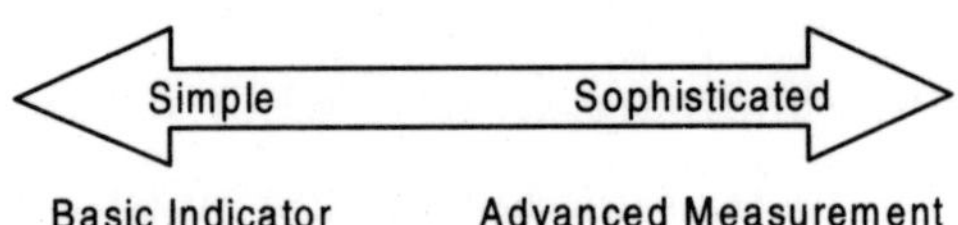

Fig. 5.1

BASIC INDICATOR APPROACH

Banks using the Basic Indicator Approach must hold capital for operational risk equal to average over the previous three years of a fixed percentage (donated alpha) of positive annual gross income. Figures for any year in which annual gross income is negative or zero, should be excluded from both the numerator and denominator when calculating the average income.

The capital charge may be expressed as follows:

$$KBIA = [\Sigma(GI1\ldots\ldots n \times \alpha)]/3$$

$$= \text{Amount for operational risk}$$

KBIA = The capital charge under the Basic Indicator Approach

GI = Annual gross income, where positive, over the pervious years

n = Number of the previous three years for which gross income is positive

α = 15 per cent which is set by the committee, relating the industry wide level of required capital to industry wide level of the indictor.

Gross income defined as net interest income plus net non-interest income. It is intended that this measure should:

(1) be gross of any provisions (e.g. for un paid interest);

(2) be gross of any operating expenses, including fees paid to outsource service providers;

(3) exclude realized profit/losses from the sale of securities in the banking book; and

(4) exclude extraordinary or irregular items as well as income derived from insurance.

Example: Calculation of operational risk under basic indicator approach

$$\textbf{KBIA} = [\Sigma(GI1 \ldots . n) \times \alpha]/3$$

KBIA = [(269,818 x 15%) + (447,619 × 15%) + (521,033 × 15%)]: 3

KBIA = [40,473 + 67,149 + 78,145] / 3 = 61,192 = Capital Charges

KBIA = 61,192 * 8 = 489,536 Total Risk Weighted

*** Gross Income (2002) = 269,818

Gross Income (2003) = 447,619

Gross Income (2004) = 521,033

STANDARDIZED APPROACH

In the Standardized Approach, Bank's activities are divided into eight business lines: corporate, finance, trading and sales, retail banking, commercial banking, payment and settlement, agency services, asset management and retail brokerage.

Within each business line, gross income is a broad indicator that serves as proxy for the scale of business operations and thus the likely scale of operational risk exposure within each of these business lines. The capital charge of each business line is calculates by multiplying gross income by a factor (denoted beta) assigned to that business line. Beta serves as proxy for the industry-wide relationship between the operational risk loss experience for given business line and the aggregate level of gross income for the business line. It should be noted that in the Standardized Approach gross income is measured for each business line, not the whole institution, i.e. in corporate finance, the indicator is the gross income generated in the corporate finance business line.

The total capital charge is calculated as the three–year average of the simple summation of the regulatory capital charges across each of the business line in each year. In any given year, negative capital charges (resulting from negative gross income) in any business line mat offset positive capital charges in other business line without limit.

However, where the aggregate capital charge across all business line within a given year is negative, then the input to the numerator for the year will be zero. The total capital charge may be expressed as:

$$KTSA = \{\Sigma_{years\ 1\text{-}3} \max [\Sigma(GI_{1\text{-}8} \times \beta_{1\text{-}8}).0]\}/3$$

Where:

KTSA = the capital charge under Standardized Approach

GI1-8 = Annual gross income in a given year, as defined above in the Basic Indicator Approach, for the each of the eight night business lines

β = A fixed percentage, set by the committee, relating the level of required capital to the level of the gross income for each of the eight business lines

The values of each business lines b are shown below:

No.	*Business Lines*	*β Factors*
1	Corporate Finance (β 1)	18%
2	Trading and Sales (β 2)	18%
3	Retail Banking (β 3)	12%
4	Commercial Banking (β 4)	15%
5	Payment and Settlement (β 5)	18%
6	Agency Services (β 6)	15%
7	Asset Management (β 7)	12%
8	Retail Banking (β 8)	12%

Source: Bank for International Settlement, Basel Committee, June 2006.

Table 5.2: Operational Risk, Standardized Approach

Business Lines	*Gross Income*			*Three Years Average*	*Beta Factor*	*Capital Charge*	*Risk Weighted Assets*
	2004	2005	2006				
Corporate Finance	130,489	136457	152918	139,955	18%	25,192	201,535
Trading and Sales	5,220	5453	6115	5,596	18%	1,007	8,058
Payment and Settlement	26,098	27291	30584	27,991	18%	5,038	40,307
Commercial Banking	104,391	109162	122334	111,962	15%	16,794	134,355
Agency Services	–	0	0	–	15%	–	–
Retail Brokerage	–	0	0	–	12%	–	–
Retail Banking	234,881	245614	275251	251,915	12%	30,230	241,839
Asset Management	20,878	21833	24467	22,393	12%	2,687	21,497
Total	521,957	545,810	611,669	559,812		80,949	647,590

Table 5.3: Operational Risk, Standardized Approach

Business Lines	Gross Income			Three Years Average	Beta Factor	Capital Charge	Risk Weighted Assets
	2004	2005	2006				
Corporate Finance	–	0	0	–	18%	–	–
Trading and Sales	–	0	0	–	18%	–	–
Payment and Settlement	130,489	136457	152918	139,955	18%	25,192	201,535
Commercial Ban-king	5,220	5453	6115	5,596	15%	839	6,715
Agency Services	26,098	27291	30584	27,991	15%	4,199	33,589
Retail Brokerage	104,391	109162	122334	111,962	12%	13,435	107,484
Retail Banking	234,881	245614	275251	251,915	12%	30,230	241,839
Asset Management	20,878	21833	24467	22,393	12%	2,687	21,497
Total	521,957	545,810	611,669	559,812		76,582	612,659

Table 5.4: Operational Risk, Standardized Approach

Business Lines	Gross Income			Three Years Average	Beta Factor	Capital Charge	Risk Weighted Assets
	2004	2005	2006				
Corporate Finance	130,489	136457	152918	139,955	18%	25,192	201,535
Trading and Sales	5,220	5453	6115	5,596	18%	1,007	8,058

(Contd.)

Payment and Settlement	26,098	27291	30584	27,991	18%	5,038	40,307
Commercial Banking	104,391	109162	122334	111,962	15%	16,794	134,355
Agency Services	234,881	245614	275251	251,915	15%	37,787	302,298
Retail Brokerage	20,878	21833	24467	22,393	12%	2,687	21,497
Retail Banking	-	0	0	-	12%	-	-
Asset Management	-	0	0	-	12%	-	-
Total	521,957	545,810	611,669	559,812		88,506	708,050

ADVANCED MEASUREMENT APPROACHES

As one can see, the gross income is the basis for calculating a capital charge for both the Basic Indicator and Standardized Approaches. In practice, these two approaches calculate the most capital charges, compared to the Advanced Measurement Approach. The Advanced Measurement Approach (AMA) is the last approach. This approach charges the least amount of capital; also this approach is comparatively more sophisticated. However, going by the sophistication of the AMA from the perspective of the cost beneficial factor, it will perhaps be wrong to conclude that it is thus far the best approach, for some banks. Consider that only large banks have the financial power to implement this approach and also make it profitable. The AMA, however, offers the greatest possibility to reduce capital requirements. It includes three approaches, namely the internal measurement approach (IMA), the scorecard approach and the Loss Distribution Approach. Read Chapter 5 for more details about the AMA Approach

The Advanced measurement approach is the most sophisticated approach currently available, presented by the Basle Committee. Under the Advanced Measurement Approaches, the calculation of the regulatory capital requirements for operational risk is based on a bank's internal risk measurement system. A bank must satisfy several criteria set out by the committee before they are permitted to use the Advanced Measurement Approach (AMA). However, within these criteria, banks are not provided with specification on distributional assumptions to generate the operational risk measure. So, banks are flexible to use any distribution to calculate the potential loss. Furthermore, on the application of these types of approaches several types of trade activities and several types of events are distinguished. These trade activities, which are referred as the eight business lines in paragraph 4.2, can be subdivided into sections. Within these sections several activities are grouped together. The mapping process is one the requirements which is set out by the Basle Committee. The difference between the AMA method and other methods is that many data are collected. Also, banks develop several methods to analyze these data to determine a reasonable amount for the regulatory capital. There are currently three sub methods available for the Advanced

Measurement Approach. The Basel Committee has identified three sub approaches to determine capital allocation for operational risk. They are: Scorecard Approach, Internal Measurement Approach, and The Loss Distribution Approach

MORE ON THE VARIOUS SUBSETS OF AMA

Accordingly, the Advanced Measurement Approach (AMA) has three broad types to choose from. They are Internal Measurement Approach, Scorecard Approach, and Loss Distribution Approach. The financial establishments have to question which approach would lead them to a lower capital charge and at the same time if it will be accepted by the regulating bodies as a sound system. It is not easy to say why each one of them would have a specific benefit to those who implement them, as it is possible each one of them could avail different benefits to those who use them to arrive at the lowest possible capital charge that is very close to the reality and appropriate (Quick 3-12)

FEATURES OF THE INTERNAL MEASUREMENT APPROACH (IMA)

One of the features of IMA is it is risk sensitive and it is possible for banks to compare its implication among themselves. What this means is each bank could retain its discretion to use its own internal loss data to reflect its own risk profile while at the same time it is possible to create some kind of uniformity as to how to calculate the capital charge among the banks involved and that can be accomplished by the supervisors that should be made up from all banks involved.

When banks use the IMA to calculate the operational risk they would start by estimating the Expected Loss Amount (ELA) for the cell they have prepared in the matrix of each business lines and event types. It is possible to do so by coming up with Exposure Indicator (EI) for each business line and it is possible to estimate the Probability of Loss Event (PE) and Loss Given Event (LGE) for the combination of the chosen business lines and loss event type. Hence, what will create ELA is the coming together of EI, PE, and LGE. To arrive at the capital required for each business line and event type there is a need to multiply the ELA by a gamma factor, which could be different across the various business lines, but should be the same across firms if there is a drive to create some kind of across-the-board-uniformity. Another proposal is using Risk Profile Index (RPI) so that it is possible to capture the loss distribution of the individual banks involved and the final capital charge would be the summation of all the products involved.

While using IMA, banks are encouraged to come up with a business line categorization system. The reason for that is when it is time to collect loss data it will be easier to do it by business line. The regulation set out by Basel II comes up with its own business line category, yet banks can use their own category by mapping out their own business involvement into standardized business lines. IMA is similar to the other methods in that it can use its own loss data to arrive at the ELA and all that is required to arrive at the ELA is EI, PE, and LGE. Another element Exposure Indicator (EI) is a proxy for the kind of operation risk exposure that is prevalent. The only requirement is since EI should be chosen carefully since it will have to be applied to all business lines. The expected loss ratio is what is going to accrue as an expected loss amount to the exposure indicator.

It is possible to decompose ELA into EI, PE, and LGE. One key issue here is certain event does not require a transaction amount attached to them, where a good example is natural disaster. Hence, it is possible to directly arrive at the ELA rather than taking the route of decomposing it into PE and LGE. The requirement dictates that when a bank is estimating the PE and LGE of its available business lines and the correlated event type combination, the primary source should be internal loss data. When it comes to standardizing the process to arrive at a parameter, supervisors could introduce methods that could exclude certain data for reasons such as it is an extreme sample or they can also introduce a safety buffer. The recommendation is to include external data if there is a need or to make the assessment forward looking. As it is applicable in the other modeless whenever there is a lack of adequate internal loss data the IMA model could also use external data and it will be the job of the supervisors to come up with standardized rules how to incorporate external data with whatever is available from within. The following examples show the capital charge calculation process using the Internal Measurement Approach:

<table>
<tr><td>Names</td><td colspan="2">Current Accord</td><td>Standardised approach</td><td>Internal Ratings Based approach</td><td>Credit Risk Modeling approach</td></tr>
<tr><td colspan="6">Operation Risk</td></tr>
<tr><td>Names</td><td colspan="2">Top-down approach: (Allocate a certain proportion of current capital to ope. Risk</td><td colspan="3">Bottom-up approach: (Estimate operational risk based on actual internal loss data)</td></tr>
<tr><td></td><td>Basic Indicator approach</td><td>Standarised approach</td><td>Internal Measurement approach</td><td>Loss Distribution approach</td><td>Modelling approach</td></tr>
<tr><td rowspan="2">Business lines and risk types</td><td rowspan="2">Single business line</td><td>Multiple business line</td><td colspan="3">Multiple business lines and event types</td></tr>
<tr><td colspan="2">Standardised by supervisors</td><td colspan="2">Bank discretion</td></tr>
<tr><td>Structure</td><td colspan="3">Σ{Cofficient * indicators}</td><td colspan="2" rowspan="4">Estimate operation VaR based on frequency and severity distributions</td></tr>
<tr><td rowspan="3">Parameters to be input</td><td rowspan="2">One exposure indicator (EI)</td><td colspan="2">Multiple Els by business lines</td></tr>
<tr><td></td><td>PE, LGE and RPI</td></tr>
<tr><td colspan="3">Standardised by supervisors</td></tr>
</table>

Source: BOJ.

		Event type A	event type B	event type c	event type D	Total
Business line A	Expected Loss (= EI*PE*LGE)	8	10	6	6	30
	Gamma Factor	5	2	5	10	
	RPI	1.0	1.0	1.6	0.7	
	Capital Charge	40	20	48	42	150
Business line B						
						100
:	:					
Total						600

Source: BOJ.

Investment banking	Corporate finance
	Trading & sales
Banking	Retail banking
	Commercial banking
	Payment & settlement
	Agency services
Others	Asset management
	Retail brokerage
	(Insurance)

Source: BOJ.

It is also possible to employ the following simple formulas to calculate the ELA using IMA, banks should provide EI, PE, and LGE.

$$\begin{aligned} ELA(i, j) &= EI(i, j) * ELR(i, j) \\ &= EI(i, j) * PE(i, j) * LGE(i, j) \end{aligned}$$

EI : Exposure Indicator

ELR : Expected Loss Ratio

PE : Probability of loss Event

LGE : Loss Given Event

It is also possible to use numbers as follows to show the relationship of the parameters.

Transactions

	Number		Amount	Losses	Number		Amount
	1	*	20		1	*	10
	1	*	20				
	1	*	10				
Total	3		60	Total	1		10
Average			20	Average			10
Gross income		=	3				
Asset size		=	600				
Number of accounts		=	6				

Source: BOJ.

Defining EI based on "flow" of business activities could be as follows:

(Case 1) • Example of business lines: Payment and settlement, etc.

• ***Example of Definition of Parameters:***

EI = volume of transactions = 60

PE = the number of loss events/the number of transactions = 1/3

LGE = average loss amount per event/average volume per transaction = 10/20

- Then, EI * PE * LGE = 60 * 1/3 * 10/20 = 10 = total loss amount

(Case 2) defining EI based on "revenue" of business activities

- ***Example of business lines: Investment banking, etc.***
- ***Example of definition of parameters: EI = gross income = 3***

PE = the number of loss events/the number of transactions = 1/3

LGE = average loss amount per event/average gross income per transaction = 10/1

- Then, EI * PE * LGE = 3 * 1/3 * 10/1 = 10 = total loss amount

(Case 3) • defining EI based on "outstanding balance" of business activities:

- ***Example of business lines: Asset management, etc***
- ***Example of definition of parameters:***

EI = value of assets under management = 600

PE = the number of loss events/the number of accounts = 1/6

LGE = average loss amount per event/average asset value per account = 10/100

• Then, EI * PE * LGE = 600 * 1/6 * 10/100 = 10 = total loss amount

Key element to look at while incorporating external data in a simple formula could look as follows:

PE = W * PE (internal) + (1-W) * PE (industry)

The W represents whatever weighting factor is used and it is supervisors who should specify it. There is a need for some kind of a minimum level or floor in IMA for the PE and LGE so that it would be possible to introduce a conservative estimate in arriving at the capital charge. Another point held high by those who prefer to use the scorecard approach is there is no tool in the other models to incorporate in the basement mechanism if there had been an improvement in risk management system. That is true here simply because the historical mean of PE and LGE cannot predict what the future PE and LGE is going to look like. Hence, in the case of IMA there is a quality adjustment to incorporate as an adjustment while trying to arrive at the capital charge. It is the job of the supervisors that should discuss it with the industry so that it will not be absent from the assessment process (Bank of Japan).

SCORECARD APPROACH

Those who support the scorecard approach is the better choice claim that it would avail a more complete and accurate measurement of what kind of operational risk would be prevalent in a given firm (PA Consulting). They also claim that this particular method avails better incentives and tool managers can use to reduce their loss, and to introduce a more practical and flexible implementation path (Chorafas 21). Accordingly, those who chose scorecard over the other methods claim that they have seen a substantial benefit, as well it was possible to introduce what they call a strong "risk culture" and have seen higher return on shareholders' interest.

What is at stake here is a sizeable amount that could be garnered by simply using AMA that is allowed to use 75 percent of what is arrived at as capital charge than using the Standardized Approach that calculates the operational risk on the 15 percent of a given bank's operating capital. The future of the floor is not certain where there is a possibility that it would either be reduced or could be eliminated as the regulators become more confident with the model the banks will be using as being effective. Till then what is going to happen is if any of the bigger banks that have up to $1 billion capital are able to reduce their capital charge at least three percent using any of the AMA methods that could be translated into several million dollars that had started accruing starting from 2005. Consequently, until new advanced operational risk measuring models come to the fore, using the AMA approach avails advantages. One of the advantages of using AMA is firms could have at least three methods to choose from if they want to put AMA to work for them.

The Internal Modeling Approach discussed above uses losses incurred on the available business lines by relying on the average past losses experienced and that could be multiplied by a gamma factor in order to arrive at the capital charge that will be applicable. The Loss Distribution Approach (LDA) works by introducing statistical distribution in the available historical loss data and arrives at the capital requirement to cover operational risk, by making numerous comparisons shown on the third section of this paper. The scoreboard approach discussed in this section uses the same method of analyzing historical loss data, but it parts with the other two methods when it starts introducing quantitative indicators about the direction the future operational risk would take. It bases its assumption on internal factors that do not have anything to do directly with loss data history, such as the kind of staff turnover that is prevalent, the kind of failure causality the system had encountered, and what kind of environment is in place. Consequently, it is up to each bank to decide which one would enable it to arrive at a lesser capital charge, while at the same time satisfying the regulators' requirements (World Bank).

Those who support the scorecard approach as the best method to implement claim that it can measure operational risk better than the other approaches, as it relies at forward-looking risk indicators, in addition to assessing the environment qualitatively. It also has a better capability by availing intensives for the managers to reduce risks and it will avail a much better tool. Especially banks that cannot put their hand on an adequate historical loss data could use scorecard method to arrive correctly at the required capital charge. It is also said to be the better situated one among the others to make the adjustments required easily, when the requirement of the regulators, as well as the banks evolve in the future.

Below there is a table that will demonstrate how scoreboard is much better in giving estimate of future loss based on whatever historical data is available by making a simple comparison with the other models.

Types of data Included in different AMA models			
	Types of Data Included		
Model	*Historical loss data*	*Quantitative risk indicators*	*Qualitative control assessments*
Internal Modeling Approach	√	√	√
Loss Distribution Approach	√	√	√
Scorecard Approach	√	√	√

Source: PA Consulting.

What this shows is the scorecard could take the assessment a notch further and includes quantitative risk indicators, as well as qualitative control assessments. Accordingly, relying heavily on historical data would lead to a failure by not being able to predict losses that could occur in the future, whereas the scorecard dependence on the quantitative, as well as qualitative risk indicators would enable it to asses that in advance. Another fallout of the other methods according to the supporters of this method is historical data fails to adopt to recent changes since it does not have link with the environment because the environment is not part of its focus, as it is for the scorecard. What this means is a bank could react to any earlier loss by tightening control so that it will not occur again. Furthermore, it is possible the bank could have introduced new products, markets, technologies, or might have come up with a different way of doing things that will not be reflected in the historical data, although all of them have a certain amount of risk exposure that will not be reflected in the historical data analysis. To make things worse, while the distribution of the risk might be the same, when it happens it could be in a different form, not covered or anticipated in the risk analysis. This is a strong argument and there is a good example the opponents cited to show the scorecard has an inherent mechanism to address such issues while measuring the premises and security risks. They claim that it is possible to examine where the crime rate stands in a given community and what kind of measures the bank had introduced. While doing the assessment, if the scorecard method encounters any new change it could immediately introduce it into the prediction, whereas the historical data users will take them years to encounter this incident and whatever they introduce would not be effective.

The scorecard method also has its opponents that claim what they call risk drivers and the weight attached to each one of them used on the scorecard are subjective, simply because it is not possible to know what each factors could be and what key role each one them could play. The supporters of the scorecard who are using also historical data admits that one way to find the relationship of the factors used in such events and business lines is by testing trends over many years. Nevertheless, the point they make is, in the meantime there are factors that indicate what the operational risk in the short term will be that are missing from the other methods. Good example cited is if there is a high turnover of staff that will lead to inexperienced staff running things in a given bank, it is not difficult to tell the risk will be higher at the particular bank when compared to another bank where the turnover is low and it is experienced staff who are running things. Hence, the problem will be using both IMA and LDA could not be effective as they are anchored in the past and do not have yet mechanisms that will enable them to look at what is happening in the immediate future. However, it is possible to defy this claim by highlighting the fact that scenario analysis is part of the LDA framework would mean that the experts could be aware of such things and whatever they recommend goes into the LDA model and that will give it robustness.

Another area scorecard supporters highlighted is it avails stronger incentives and better tools for managers to deal with operational risks. Accordingly, the point again stresses that the other methods' use of historical data pattern to assess the risks could take many years and any kind of reduction introduced could not result in an immediate lower capital charge allocation. This could result in depriving managers to integrate into their assessment any short-term changes in the staff, systems, or process. As a result, the case of the scorecard is different in such a way that it is possible to create an immediate linkage between measures that could mitigate risks and that will lead to capital charge reductions. The implication of such an understanding would be there is no need to wait for many years in order to introduce a change in the environment.

Again, this could be defied simply because such measures are part of the LDA analysis for example, as it will be shown in the next section, since the model incorporates experts advice and suggestions in such a way that the capital charge arrived at will include these current problems and trends. Yet, the fact that scorecard could allow the managers to take measures according to the findings might be one of its advantages, simply because the incentive to make managers take immediate measures to reduce risk might be absent from both methods as both are heavily reliant on historical loss data, turning to scenario analysis when there is a shortage only. Furthermore, the scorecard proponents highlight that the incentive tools available in the method could make a big difference since managers do not have to wait for years at times to introduce measures that will mitigate risk simply because both methods do not have a mechanism that will make the mangers take immediate measures to reduce risk.

Another point raised was the "what-if" question issue where the presumption is to enable managers to take immediate action on their findings if there is a need to introduce measures that will mitigate risk reduction. That capability is also available in the scenario analysis of LDA and it is up to managers to evaluate which method will be effective for what they are doing since AMA is open for the decision of those in charge where the only requirement is to meet the regulators requirement at the end. Overall what the scorecard approach would avail is a two throng capability where on the one hand it will be possible to arrive accurately as to what the capital charge should be based on the findings, and while on the other it is possible to introduce changes if not for what happened, but for what will happen in the future that will start immediately.

Another advantage highlighted is the ease and flexibility the mode avails while implementing it. It is neither expensive, unnecessarily difficult, nor, time consuming when compared with the other two methods and that is in addition to its being more flexible than the others for changes that would occur over time. The table below shows comparatively why the other AMA models fall short and are difficult to implement. Even if all methods require data, the data scorecard method is dependant upon is not historical that require to go back up to five years, instead it is data well-run banks keep as part of their current operations.

Model	*Implementation Factors*				
	Time	*Cost*	*Need for loss data*	*Need for resources*	*Management buy-in*
Internal Modeling Approach	Medium	Low to medium	Large	Small	Low
Loss Distribution Approach	Long	Medium to high	Very large	Medium	Very low
Scorecard Approach	Short to medium	Medium to high	Medium	Large	High

Source: PA Consulting.

Fig. 5.2: Implementation factors in different AMA models

Furthermore, when looking at the time and the cost involved scorecard might be less expensive for the banks that implement it. However, when looking at the work process the scorecard might be more involving and require more staff than the other two models that can be handled by a centralized team that is made up of fewer staff since the major task is collecting data. Scorecard method could involve not only many experts, but also all business units might have to participate in constructing the scorecard, which could end up involving a big number of people. In spite of all this, the main advantage highlighted is what is labeled as "management buy-in" where there is a failure in the part of the management to understand or trust the statistical model applied in both IMA and LDA approaches. Also it is not possible to visualize how it will enable the management team to run their business effectively so that things will be different for the coming years as both systems are focusing on the amount of capital charge involved, where if they bring it down, it would mean they have done a good job. What the scorecard approach brings to the fore is its common sense approach, inputs that are easily recognizable, and an immediate feedback that requires action, which makes it better suited for the banks. The following table demonstrates how the scorecard approach is much easier as far as adapting to conditions that are changing over-time is concerned.

Type of change	Loss history-based approach (IMA /LDA)	Scorecard approach
New Business Line (eg by acquisition)	Need to collect loss history for this business—may take years if this is not immediately available	Scorecards can be applied immediately if basic data available—should take only weeks/months
New type of risk (eg e-commerce related)	Need to collect loss history for this risk—may take years if this is not immediately available	New scorecard can be developed in weeks/months based on common sense and available data
Additional Data Source identified	Can be incorporated if data is loss history	Can be incorporated, whatever the type of data
More advanced Model Developed (eg causal modeling)	Advanced model can replace loss data approach for one or more business lines	Advanced model can replace scorecard approach for one or more business lines

Source: PA Consulting.

Fig. 5.3: Response of AMA models to changes in environment

Even if scorecard model is as new as the other AMA approaches, it had been in use in some banks for some time now and the findings are:

- It was possible to reduce risk and losses identified using the scorecard model that had proven to be profitable;
- The introduction of a much fortified risk management

culture where top-bottom involvement had got enhancement;

- To be in apposition to introduce a better risk control environment that leads to a better return on stock markets;

PRACTICAL USE OF LOSS DISTRIBUTION APPROACH

The origin of quantitative Loss Distribution Approach (LDA) goes back to the insurance industry that had been using it for a long time. However, although it was in practical use by an industry, it was not simple enough to incorporate directly to assessing operational risks without first dealing with the bias that will come into existence. Furthermore, since the availability of such data is small comparatively to others, it had made it difficult to base the operation risk basement solely on LDA. In reality, it is possible to apply a full operational risk assessment based on LDA and reconcile both the quantitative and qualitative points to arrive at a more accurate capital charge. There are several steps involved in accomplishing that and each one of them requires a close look in order to implement theme effectively (GRO). They are:

- Severity Estimation
- Frequency Estimation
- Capital Charge Computations

- Confidence Interval
- Self Basement and Scenario analysis

SEVERITY ESTIMATION

Severity estimation is one of the steps and it is always difficult to manipulate simply because there is always bias to deal with. As a result, there will be a conflict between accuracy and simplicity because of the fact that it is not possible to treat data according to some set of rules, without being unbiased, hence there is no avoiding the introduction of some complexity to do a much accurate assessment of the severity. One step to take would be to scale the available data if it is obtained from external source, simply because the source of the data might not be similar to the firm that acquired it and it requires to be scaled in order to be used. The other possibility is if the source of the data is from a similar source and all that is required is integrating it, there is no need for scaling as it fits without introducing any high scale bias and this paper had covered this issue earlier. However, when looking at the complexity the data that requires scaling will avail, it is a complicated challenge simply because there is some work involved before putting it to work.

Another problem that would be prevalent could be, while scaling an external data so that it will incorporate with internal data without introducing bias, it is possible to face a problem of coming up with different formulas for each source, simply because one formula might not work across the board. A much worse case scenario is it is possible that there could be a conflict between two business lines of the same establishment require to introduce different formulas making the work more complex and difficult. Therefore, the point to highlight here is when dealing with severity issue, it is possible to avoid the complication by simply reporting the prevalent bias and that could make the task of assessing the severity less complex and more accurate.

What plays a key role in severity distribution is the threshold because that is what the reported losses are going to be based upon. However, there is an element called the "true one" which is the result arrived at if all losses were reported without a threshold, and in reality that is what should be used to arrive at the correct capital charge. Because of that, there is a need to link the distribution, as much as possible to the true one. To solve this problem it is possible to use Maximum Likelihood (ML) ratio simply because this approach is widely acknowledged by the likes of (Baud, Rachot, and Roncalli, 2002 and Fontnouvell et al. 2003) as they are among the authorities on the subject as discussed in the literature. The former batch of these authorities had proven that if reporting bias is not included, whatever arrived at would not be near to what is acceptable as accurate. It is not difficult to see the problem here as simply mentioning that if a data loss is from outside sources that are using different threshold, there is a need to address the bias that will be prevalent.

There is a mathematical calibration where it is possible to use the log likelihood function where the parameters are as follows:

μ and α

The function would look like as follows:

$$\max_{(\mu,\alpha)} l_n(\mu,\alpha) = \sum_{i=1}^{n} l(\zeta i,\mu,\alpha|H_i)$$

where n is the number of losses, $l(\zeta i,\mu,\alpha|H_i)$ is the loglikelihood of the ith loss (reported subject to the threshold H_i)

Source: (GRO).

FREQUENCY ESTIMATION

Frequency distribution might be the simplest process simply because what is looked at is the average number of events per year, as that is what its Maximum Likelihood value is. Still bias arising mostly from the kind of threshold used could affect making bias reporting an important part of the process. What this implies to is a firm that is using a higher threshold could end up reporting less frequency and that does not necessarily mean such a firm should put aside a lower capital charge than another firm that uses a lower threshold ending up with higher frequencies count and that would force a firm to put aside a larger capital charge. A simple way out from this problem again is reporting the bias so that it would be possible to correct the number of events. At the same time the "true" element could work in frequency estimation case, since it is the capital charge arrived at without using a threshold. There is a simply formula to show this and it looks like as follows:

$$\lambda = \frac{\lambda_{sample}}{\Pr\{loss > H\}}$$

which is the mathematically equal to:

$$\lambda = \frac{\lambda_{sample}}{1 - F(H; \mu, \sigma)}$$

In practical terms, one has to complete the average number of reported events by year (which is an estimate of l_{sample}) and to use the previous estimates of m and s to uncover the untrue frequency distribution.

Source: (GRO).

WHAT IS INVOLVED WHILE SCALING DATA

What is the key when it comes to scaling data is the prevalent link used between any of the available variables, where in some cases by simply taking a square root of the available data will be possible to scale it for use. Example used is the number of events in a bank, for example, could be the square root of its business volume. The finding is, as far as the use of frequency of data is concerned, arriving at the correct capital charge could not be reliable simply because it is possible that there will be a lack of data to check for such links thoroughly and arrive at a meaningful figure that could be incorporated into what would lead to arriving at the correct capital charge. There is even a suggestion that taking frequencies of data loss for granted might be advisable simply because the amount of data that will be available to make the assessment might not be enough to make it a good measuring tool.

FRAUD RISK INCREASING RAPIDLY

The average larger company loss to fraud has increased by 22 percent largely driven by the credit crunch and tough economic climate, according to the latest Kroll Global Fraud Report. Companies lost an average of $8.2 million to fraud in the past three years, compared to last year's figure which stood at $7.6 million. The figures are a result of a survey Kroll commissioned from the Economist Intelligence Unit of 890 senior executives worldwide.

The fastest growing types of fraud were information theft (27 percent: up from 22 percent) and regulatory and compliance breaches (25 percent: up from 19%), both up by more than five percentage points from last year's survey.

(www.kroll.com/fraud) (17th Sept 2008)

CAPITAL CHARGE

Capital charge is 99.9 percentile of the total loss distribution arrived at. Alternatively, it is possible to define it by incorporating the threshold in the loss distribution, where capital charge is the overall total less the distribution factor arrived at after introducing a threshold; hence, the 99.9 percent of the loss distribution above the threshold could be the capital charge. Consequently, capital charge is the amount a bank should put aside to cover operational risks and it does not matter how it is arrived at, as various methods are allowed as long as they satisfy the regulators, although the process is heavily dependant on loss data, as well as the kind of threshold introduced. It is not, however, meant to water down the vital role the threshold is playing, simply because where the threshold is marked would indicate what kind of capital charge would be arrived at. It is not only that the two components discussed earlier, the severity and frequency of losses are the outcome of where the point of the threshold is marked. The simplest method of arriving at the capital charge looks at 99.9 percentile of the total loss distribution and it is possible to show it mathematically as follows.

$$L = \sum_{i=0}^{N} \zeta_i$$

$$\Pr\{L > OpVaR\} = 0.1\%$$

Source: (GRO).

AGGREGATING LOSSES TO ARRIVE AT CAPITAL CHARGE

The first point to consider is it is not easy to categorize aggregate loss data by the kind of risk type it will be causing or it is not possible to correlate aggregate losses to the kind of risk they could introduce. Naturally, capital charge is arrived at by looking at the randomness nature of the frequency and severity (Chernobai, Menn, and Rachev (30)2. It is possible to take fraud as an example assuming that the aggregate data could be the outcome of both internal and external data. There could be a correlation here simply because it is possible to look at the severity as well as the frequency and draw some correlation. It is possible to assume that when the external fraud loss is high the possibility is that the internal fraud loss could also be high, simply because that had been the reality across the industry. This might be the correct way of looking at similar event types that have different sources. There is a mathematical formula that shades a light on what takes place in various aggregate loss data where the parameter could be similar.

Let us consider two aggregate losses $L_1 = \sum_{i=0}^{N_1} \zeta_i^1$ and $L_2 = \sum_{i=0}^{N_2} \zeta_i^2$. In order to obtain tractable formula, we assume that the two frequency distributions have the same parameters $\lambda_1 = \lambda_2 = \lambda$. If N_1 and N_2 are perfectly correlated, it comes that $N_1 = N_2 = N$. We have

Source: (GRO).

It is possible to do a calculation based on this, but this itself will serve to demonstrate what it means by frequency-correlation that does not necessarily lead to correlating among aggregate loses, where there will be a need to introduce diversification in order to arrive at a lower capital charge.

CONFIDENCE INTERVAL

Capital charge is not something to arrive at with any high degree of certainty and the regulators expect it to be as closer as possible to the true picture of the risk that would be involved. Nevertheless, it is possible that there could be some difficulty to contend with what will come into existence, simply because there is always a shortage of historical loss data. Therefore, there had come into existence a need for a tool that justifies the involved process is much closer to reality.

If there is another factor that will affect the accuracy of the capital charge, it could be the kind of parameters used. The best way to approach this problem is to construct would be underlying estimators to be used and try to come up with as many simulations as possible, and for each path it would be possible to compute the would be capital charge. This is when there is a need to introduce material calculation that would use various kinds of formulas to arrive at the best possible capital charge. By doing that it might be possible to arrive at a correct estimate of the capital charge, while it is also possible to introduce graphs in order to track correctly at what points the most appropriate capital charge could be spotted.

LOOKING AT SELF ASSESSMENT AND SCENARIO ANALYSIS

When giving consideration to scenario analysis the assumption is bank experts and managers have a good understanding of the kind of risk they could be dealing with, and reflecting these expertise and understanding from data collected in whatever form they are is not easy. Because of that it is a good work practice to let these experts and mangers have a say about the capital charge that is arrived at, and then it will be possible to incorporate the findings into the severity and frequency data loss used to asses the capital charge. It is possible to accomplish that by scenario building where it is possible for experts to make suggestions on what kind of losses incurred in a given time-span. When that is the case, such a suggestion could be useful if there is a shortage of loss data or if the compiled data is not forward looking.

The point to raise here is it is possible to incorporate such findings into an LDA framework effectively and the end result could be arriving at a more appropriate capital charge. It is possible to do that by using a mathematical formula that uses frequency and severity distribution parameters. The crucial point is to recognize the restriction and once that is accomplished what comes next is designing a calibration strategy where introducing some standard criterion such as Maximum Likelihood would be possible. The end result of such introduction could be a parameter estimator could play the dual role of introducing advice in the assessment of both loss-data estimator and scenario-based estimator. The following source demonstrates how that is possible.

Let us *consider a scenario defined* as: "a *loss of x or higher occurs once* every *d* years". *Let us also assume that* the *frequency distribution is a Poisson* district (with parameter λ) *and that the severity distribution is a lognormal distribution (with parameters* μ, *and* σ*). With these notations,* λ *is the average number of losses* per year, λ × (1 - F(*x*; μ, σ) is *the* average *number of losses higher than x and finally* $\frac{1}{\lambda \times (1 - F(x;\mu,\sigma))}$ *is the average duration*[3] *between two losses exceeding x. As a result, jor a given scenario (x, d), parameters are restricted to satisfy:*

Source: Groupe de Recherche Op´erationnelle.

References

1. AMA FDIC" "Supervisory Guidance for ORM", http://www.fdic.gov/regulations/laws/publiccomments/basel/oprisk.pdf.

2. APEC "Bank Governance Principles and Basel 2" http://www.apec-finsecreg.org/bankgovernance.htm

3. Bank of Japan "Advancing ORM" www.boj.or.jp/en/type/release/zuiji_new/fsc0608c.pdf

4. ORM Systems CHARTIS www.chartis-research.com

5. Bank of Japan "Discussions on Further Advancing Operational Risk Management" www.boj.or.jp/en/type/release/zuiji_new/fsc0608c.pdf

6. Bank of Japan "Internal Measurement Approach to Operational Risk Capital Charge"
www.boj.or.jp/en/type/ronbun/ron/wps/kako/data/fwp01e02.pdf

7. BIS "Range of Practice in Banks' Internal Ratings Systems" www.bis.org/publ/bcbs66.pdf

8. BIS "The importance of transparency and market discipline approaches in the New Capital Accord" http://www.bis.org/review/r031112b.pdf

9. BITS "Financial Services Developing a KRI Programme"

http://www.bitsinfo.org/downloads/Publications%20Page/bitskriprog.doc.

10. Boudoukh, Jacob, Mathew Richanrtson, and Robert Whitelaw, 1995, "Expect the Worst." RISK 8, no. 9 pp. 101.

11. Calomiris, Charles, and Richard, Herring. 2002, "The Regulation of Operational Risk in Investment Management Companies, Perspective, Investment Company. Institute", pp. 1-19.

12. Chernobai, A., Menn C., and Rachev S.T., "Note on the Estimation of the Frequency and Severity Distribution of Operational Losses", the Mathematical Scientist, 30 (2).

13. Chorafas, Dimitris N. "Operational Risk Control with Basel II: Basic Principles and Capital Requirements", Elsiver Butterworth, UK.

14. Continuity Central "Measuring operational risk management systems under Basel II"

    www.03.ibm.com/industries/financialservices/doc/content/resource/te chnical/1897889103.html

15. Currie, Carolyn "Basel II and Operational Risk: An Overview", Risk Books, 2004.

16. Cummins, J.D., C.M. Lewis, and R. Wei. 2006. "The Market Value Impact of Operational Loss Events for U.S. Banks and Insurers." Journal of Banking and Finance 30(10).

17. D'Agostino, Ralph B. and Michael A. Stephens, "Goodness-of-Fit Techniques", New York, NY: Marcel Dekker, Inc. 1986.

18. De Fontnouvelle, P.V. DeJesus-Rueff, J.S. Jordan, and E.S. Rosengren, 2006. "Capital and Risk: New Evidence on the Implications of Large Operational Losses." Journal of Money, Credit, and Banking 38(7) (October) pp. 1,819-1,846.

19. De Fontnouvelle, Patrick, John S. Jordan, and Eric S. Rosengren, "Implications of Alternative Operational Risk Modeling Techniques," NBER Working Paper No. W1103.

20. Federal Reserve Bank Boston "Using Loss Data to Quantify Operational Risk" www.bis.org/bcbs/events/wkshop0303/p04deforose.pdf

21. Federal Reserve Board "Exploring Costs, Capital Requirements and Risk Mitigation"
www.federalreserve.gov/SECRS/2007/July/20070717/OP-1277/OP-1277_16_1.pdf

22. Financier Transforming Data into knowledge"
http:// wwwarcl.co.uk /financier _ww_may_ 07_Final.pdf.

23. Fitch "Ratings Financial Institutions" www.fitch.fr/pdf/rapports/eta_rap_34

24. FRBNY "The Challenges of Risk Management in Diversified Financial Companies" http://www.ny.frb.org/research/epr/01v07n1/0103cumm.html

25. Groupe de Recherche Op´erationnelle (GRO) "Loss Distribution Approach in Practice"

www.gro.creditlyonnais.fr/content/wp/lda-practice.pdf

26. Froot, Kenneth A., "Bank Capital and Risk Management: Operational Risks In Context," 2003. Presentation at the Federal Reserve Bank of Boston.

27. Holmquist, Eric. "Right-Sizing ORM: Scaling Operational Risk Management for the Small and Medium-Sized Market", Risk Books

28. Hull, John C. "Risk Management and Financial Institutions", Prentice Hall, 2006.

IBM "Operational Risk Management and IT" www-03.ibm.com/industries/financialservices/doc/content/resource/technica l/1897889103.html

29. IMF "Operational Risk: The Sting is Still in the Tail, but the Poison Depends on the Dose" http://www.imf.org/external/pubs/ft/wp/2007/wp07239.pdf.

30. IMF "Operational Risk and Reference Data: Exploring Costs, Capital Requirements and Risk Mitigation" http://www.imf.org/external/pubs/ft/wp/2007/wp07254.pdf.

31. Kaiser, Thomas, and Köhne, Marc. "An Introduction to Operational Risk", Risk Books.

32. Knowledge Leader "Basel II yields increased focus on managing operational risk" www.knowledgeleader.com/KnowledgeLeader/Content.nsf/Web+Con tent/HotIssuesBaseII

33. Koker, Rudi De. "Operational Risk Modelling: Where Do We Go From Here? The Advanced Measurement Approach to Operational Risk" 37-57. London: Risk books.

34. Lawyers Weekly Online "Basel II Continues to Cause Concern" www.lawyersweeklyonline.com/au/articles/Basel-II-continues-to-cause-concerns_z7055.htm

35. Moscaeli, Macro, "The Modeling of Operational Risk: Experience with the Analysis of the Data Collected by the Basel Committee," 2004 Working Paper.

36. NYFRB EPR "Evaluation of Value-at-Risk Models Using Historical Data" NYFRB Economic Review April 1996 Volume 2, Number 1, http://www.ny.frb.org/research/epr /epr/96v02n1/9604hend.pdf

37. New York Federal "An LDA-Based AMA for the Measurement of OR" www.newyorkfed.org/newsevents/events/banking/2003/con0529p.pdf

38. New York Federal "Scenario-Based AMA" www.newyorkfed.org/newsevents/events/banking/2003/con0529d.pdf

39. Oliver Wyman Consulting "The Evolving Role of the Chief Financial Officer and the Chief Risk Officer" http://www.merceroliverwyman.com/perspectives/articles/owc_nov_02_the_evolving_role_of_the_cfo_and_cro-executive%20summary.pdf

40. PA Consulting "Choose Your Weapons...Moving forward on Operational Risk in the Light of the New Basel Accord". www.paconsulting.com/news/by_pa/2001/by_pa200111010.htm

41. Quick, Jeremy. (2006) "The Advanced Measurement Approach: Getting It Started". 3-13. London: Risk books.

42. Rachev, T., Fabozz, Frank. Chernobai, A., "Operational Risk: A Guide to Basel II Capital Requirements, Models, and Analysis", John Wiley & Sons Inc, New York, 2006.

43. Resilience Engineering "The Art of Striking the Balance between Risk Mitigation and Creating Policies" http://www.resilience-engineering.org/REPapers/Sundstrom_Hollnagel.pdf

44. Risk management Magazine "Risk Management in Practice: Internal Control within the Financial Establishments" www.riskmanagementmagazine.com.au/articles/51/0C038B51.asp?

45. RWTH "Improving Operation Management Systems" http://ftp.informatik.rwth-aachen.de/Publications/CEUR-WS/Vol-241/paper8.pdf.

46. ULM "A Tale of Tails" www.mathematik.uni-ulm.de/finmath/courses/ws0607/operational.Risk/dutta.pdf

47. Wharton "The Key to Risk Management" http://fic.wharton.upenn.edu/fic/papers/99/9942.Pdf

48. World Bank "Bank Regulation and Supervision: What Works Best" http://www.worldbank.org/research/interest/prr_stuff/wwb_122001.pdf

Index